Urban Identity

Urban Identity is the second in the successful Learning from Place series that draws upon the wealth of experience in The Academy of Urbanism. This editions deals with the subject of urban identity and character. Why is it that all modern towns and cities look the same, as they become dominated by identikit buildings, multi-national corporations, even arbitrarily imposed urban design rules. How can we preserve and foster the sense of local identity and character that so value without falling into the trap of historical pastiche?

Four leading urban thinkers take this theme as the starting point for chapters on urban identity. The classical architect Robert Adam delivers a broadside to modern architecture, which he sees as the multi-national face of globalism. The Architect and academic John Worthington ponders the difference between how a place is seen, its identity and how it wants to be seen, its brand, while the architects Anthony Reddy from Ireland and Frank Walker from Scotland explore the notion of local and national identity in architecture and design.

These chapters are interspersed with five chapters by leading practitioners inspired by the shortlisted places for the Academy's second annual awards. The surveyor Chris Balch revels in the life of three great European cities while Brian Evans and Chris Brett celebrate three towns that are really great small cities. David Rudlin looks at three creative quarters and what they contribute to the economic and social life of their host cities while Frank McDonald takes us on a journey down three great streets and David Taylor and Anthony Alexander applaud three urban places created and improved in recent years.

Like the first book in this series, Urban Identity brims with fascinating and sometimes controversial insights and opinions on urbanism. Illustrated again by the drawings of David (Harry) Harrison and poems by Ian McMillan and packed with photographs and plans of the places visited by the Academy as part of their awards scheme.

The Academy of Urbanism brings together a diverse group of thinkers, decision-makers and practitioners and seeks to identify and promote best practice in urbanism.

Urban Identity

The Academy of Urbanism

Edited by Brian Evans, Frank McDonald and David Rudlin

Routledge
Taylor & Francis Group

LONDON AND NEW YORK

THE ACADEMY
OF URBANISM

First published 2011
by Routledge
2 Park Square, Milton Park, Abingdon, Oxon OX14 4RN

Simultaneously published in the USA and Canada
by Routledge 711 Third Avenue, New York, NY 10017

Routledge is an imprint of the Taylor & Francis Group, an informa business

British Library Cataloguing in Publication Data
A catalogue record for this book is available from the British Library

Library of Congress Cataloging-in-Publication Data
Urban identity : learning from place 2 / Academy of Urbanism ; edited by Brian
Evans, Frank McDonald and David Rudlin.

p. cm.
"This is the second anthology of place study published by the Academy."
1. City planning. 2. Urbanization. 3. Cities and towns. 4. Sociology, Urban. I. Evans,
B. M. (Brian M.) II. McDonald, Frank, 1950 Jan. 24- III. Rudlin, D. IV. Academy of
Urbanism (Organisation)
HT166.U7136 2011
307.76--dc22
2010050635

ISBN13: 978-0-415-61402-3 (hbk)
ISBN13: 978-0-415-61403-0 (pbk)

Typeset in Helvetica Neue LT Std by
URBED
Printed and bound in Great Britain by Ashford Colour Press Ltd

Contents

Buchanan Street Glasgow

John Thompson

Foreword

In this, the second book in the *Learning from Place* series, we bring you a further sequence of great places at the level of the City, Town, Neighbourhood, Street and Place.

All of these places form part of a seamless continuum that links their past to their present and their present to their future. They are neither old nor new. They are living organisms, reborn every day at dawn.

Each is unique and possesses a treasure-trove of embedded knowledge that has lain ignored and untapped for over a century. Preoccupied primarily with a fascination for the physical embodiment of place, what we can see and what we can touch, we have failed to show any real and sustained interest in delving beneath their surfaces to understand how their inner structures are inextricably related to their outward health and performance.

If we are to enhance civilisation and safeguard our future, we must first gain a simultaneous understanding of what lies before our eyes, under our feet and, ultimately, in our hearts.

Through UniverCities, the Academy is launching its campaign to gain a shared and proper understanding of the DNA of place through the creation of a network of urban laboratories that will be united both by a common purpose - to chronicle the physical, social, economic and environmental footprints of place, and by a common Charter - to formalize collaboration between Cities, Practice, Academia and Civic Society as they collectively pursue this common goal.

We inherit Space from the planet; we shape it to create Place; and the results either nurture or destroy Life. Through UniverCities, we invite you to join the Academy in its quest to re-unite these fundamental components of great placemaking.

John Thompson
Chairman The Academy of Urbanism

Acknowledgements

"Urban Identity" is the second anthology in the "Learning from Place" series that documents what the Academy has learned from visiting and studying the three short-listed cities, towns, neighbourhoods, streets and places. As with the first volume, this task would have been nigh impossible without the commitment, time, insight and understanding of those who are in some way responsible for the shortlisted places together with those who visited, studied and documented the shortlist in each category.

In the three cities, Drs Sabine Lebesque, Simone van Harten, Jan Hagendoorn, Dr Zef M Hemel, Charlotte Hillbrand, Jurgen Hoogendoorn, Joyce Hamilton, Jeroen M den Uyl, Clara Overes, Klaas W De Boer provided formidable knowledge and insight into Amsterdam; as did Juan Roig Vila (a special thank you for taking time out from his family holiday to show us round) in Barcelona; and Takis Panagiotis Sgouros, Mark Toennes, Peter Gollas, Astrid Tag, Ulrich Lautenschlager, Regina Beument, Barbara Berninger, Stephanie Rabb in Berlin. Tha Academy would like to thank Andreas von Zadow, Sally Saddeh and Clara Overes for co-ordinating the European trip.

With the towns, Bill Tyrell, John McCormack, Cllr Malcolm Nonnan, Cllr Betty Manning, Cllr Sean O'Hargain, Cllr John Norton, Cllr Joe Reidy, Cllr Martin Brett, Michael Brennan, Kieran Fitzgerald, Kevin Hanley, Cllr Marie Fitzpatrick, Cllr Joe Cody, Cllr Michael Lanigan, Cllr Andrew McGuinness, Cllr Paul Cuddihy, Cllr Pat Crotty, Cllr John Coonan all gave their valuable time and knowledge in Kilkenny; as did Bill Lindsay, Dily Livingston, Patrick Laughlin, Martin Grigg, John Stewart, Willie Johnston, Stephen Magee, Roddy Yarr, Niall Scott, Anne Morris, David Middleton, Robert Steedman, Lesley Barrie, John Matthews, Sarah Robertson, Bill Sangster, Peter Milne, Riccardo Marini in St. Andrews; and Cllr George Beckett, Cllr Patricia Stallard, Simon Eden, Eloise Appleby, Antonia Perkins, Eleanor Hodge, Tommy Geddes, Cllr Dominic Hiscock, Huw Thomas, Diana Wooldridge, Alan Weeks, Jim Sawyer, Robert Adam in Winchester.

Andrew Dixon, Phil Payne, Anne Howe, Peter Howe, Fiona Cullen, Jill Young, Tony Wyatt, Alan Simpson organised an excellent visit of Grainger Town; as did Lydia Clarkson, Simon Quayle, Carly Fry, Neil Hall in Soho; and Dick Gleeson, Paddy Burke, Paul Koegh, Killian Skay, Tony Reddy in Temple Bar.

Steve Inch, Hugh McKergow, Willie Caie, Gerry Grams contributed insight and passion to the Buchanan Street visit; as did Dick Gleeson, Paul Koegh, Killian Skay, Tony Reddy with O'Connell Street; and also Peter Bourne, Farrah Hassen-Hardwick, Peter Heath, Andrew Payne, Robert Seatter, Annie Walker, David Shaw in Portland Place.

Finally, Andrew Dixon, Phil Payne, Anne Howe, Peter Howe, Peter Udall, John Devil, Alan Simpson organised an insightful visit of Quayside; as did Simon Ogden, Richard Watts, Yunas Ahmed, Maura Gallagher, Tim Rippon, Andrew Sturch, James Arnold, Stewart Gulliver with Peace and Winter Gardens; and Dan Taylor, Savas Sivetidis, Alistair Huggett on the South Bank.

The Academy would like to thank Ian McMillan for his poems, David (Harry) Harrison for his sketches and Joe Wood from JTP for preparing the figure-ground drawings.

We would like to thank Linda Gledstone, Stephen Gallagher, Felicity Meerloo and Janet Sutherland for their commitment and work in support of the Academy.

Chris Balch, Chris Brett, Frank McDonald, David Taylor and Anthony Alexander for their hard work assessing the Great Places and putting the chapters together as well as Robert Adam, John Worthington, Anthony Reddy and Frank Walker for the thematic chapters.

Finally, Brian & Frank would like to give a special thank you to David Rudlin for unlocking the logjam in the graphic design and Alex Hollingworth at Routledge for taking on the publication of the series that sees this anthology and the first volume, "Space, Place, Life", published together.

Regent Street London

Contributors

Robert Adam trained at the University of Westminster and won a Rome Scholarship. He has practised in the city of Winchester since 1977 and co-founded Winchester Design in 1986, which became known as Robert Adam Architects in 2000. He works closely with clients on a diverse range of projects including major private houses, extensions to historic buildings and public and commercial buildings. He has 20 years experience in masterplanning and has pioneered objective coding. Robert's contribution to the classical tradition is internationally acknowledged, both as a scholar and as a designer of traditional and progressive classical architecture. He is also a designer of classical furniture. He founded the Popular Housing Forum in 1995 as a result of his long involvement with speculative housing and masterplanning. He was also one of the founders of the International Network for Traditional Building, Architecture & Urbanism (INTBAU) in 2000. His work is widely published, broadcast and exhibited. He writes, lectures and broadcasts on a variety of subjects including classical architecture, masterplanning, housing and countryside issues. He has also undertaken lecture tours of the USA and Russia. Robert is a founding Academician at The Academy of Urbanism.

Anthony Alexander is Director of Studies and Research at Alan Baxter and Associates. His skills range from business development to creative design, and his work in digital media and, latterly, sustainability, as well as his academic background in the philosophy of science, has centred on the introduction of new ways of thinking. He is a former Creative Director and Operations Manager, and his work promotes sustainable development. He contributed to the United Nations Earth Summit in 2002 and climate conference 2005. Anthony has written on sustainability and climate issues for the national and professional press and has contributed to textbooks and academic journals on sustainable urban design. His major work Britain's New Towns was published in 2009 (Routledge).

Professor Chris Balch is from West Somerset. He studied geography at Sidney Sussex, Cambridge and urban design and regional planning at Edinburgh University, later qualifying as a Chartered Town Planner and Surveyor. He has more than 30 years experience working in both local government and private consultancy with a particular interest in urban regeneration and large-scale development projects. He advised government on the Leeds Development Corporation in the late 1980's and subsequent proposals for Housing Action Trust in Leeds, Hull and Tower Hamlets as well as on the funding of major Millennium projects including the Lowry Arts complex at Salford Quays, the Millennium Stadium in Cardiff, the Odyssey Project in Belfast and the Forum in Norwich. Internationally he has worked in Bahrain, Malaysia, Pakistan and the Czech Republic. He was Managing Director of DTZ in the UK and Chair of Basildon Renaissance Partnership, one of the local delivery agencies in the Thames Gateway. He is now Professor of Planning at the University of Plymouth. He is a founding Academician at The Academy of Urbanism.

Chris Brett joined the Barton Willmore Planning Partnership in April 1987 as Senior Planner. He was promoted to Associate and subsequently Director. He became a partner in 1996 and is now based in the London office, in charge of urban regeneration projects. He provides advice to both public and private sector clients on all aspects of the planning and development process relating to, inter alia, major mixed-use housing, leisure and employment schemes and new settlement. Chris appears as an expert witness at public local inquiries (planning appeals), local plan inquiries, and structure plan Examinations-in-Public. He negotiates inputs into Section 106 agreements and has co-ordinated and contributed to Environmental Impact Assessments. In 1998 Chris appeared on the BBC's Panorama programme, 'Battle of the Green Belt' and in 1999 appeared on Anglia Television's 'Monday Night Extra' programme relating to the major development proposed to the west of Stevenage, for which he was lead consultant. He made representations into the Mayor for London's Spatial Strategy and gave evidence at the Examination in Public on behalf of a number of clients. Other major projects (many of which are planning causes célèbres) include Imperial Wharf Fulham and Vodafone World Head Quarters Newbury. Chris is also a Fellow of the Royal Society of the Arts and a founding Academician at The Academy of Urbanism.

Brian Evans is from St. Andrews and was educated at Edinburgh and Strathclyde universities. Since 1989, he has been a partner of Gillespies, leading landscape design and regeneration projects in the UK, Scandinavia, Russia, the Middle East and China. From 2004 until 2010, he was Deputy Chair of Architecture+Design Scotland and before that a CABE enabler. He was previously a member of the City of Sheffield's Urban Design Review Panel and is now co-chair of the City's Sustainable Development & Design Panel. He is co-author of Tomorrow's Architectural Heritage (Mainstream, 1991) and urban design adviser for Making Cities Work (Wiley, 2003). He has taught widely at architecture schools in Britain and continental Europe. From 1998 until 2004, he was Artistic Professor of Urban Design at Chalmers University School of Architecture in Gothenburg. In 2008 he was made an honorary professor at the Mackintosh School of Architecture, Glasgow School of Art and in 2010 was invited to become Head of Urbanism there. He is a co-founder and a director of The Academy of Urbanism.

David (Harry) Harrison is a Partner at John Thompson & Partners and an architect with a wide experience of urban design and community planning in both the private and public sectors, throughout the UK and Europe. His projects include award-winning schemes at Barnes Waterside and Putney Wharf in London and at Charter Quay in Kingston-upon-Thames. He is from Norwich and is The Academy of Urbanism's Artist-in-Residence and his paintings and drawings have been displayed at the Royal Academy's Summer Exhibition.

Frank McDonald is from Dublin and lives in Temple Bar, the city's 'cultural quarter'. Educated at St Vincent's CBS Glasnevin and University College Dublin, he is Environment Editor of The Irish Times, having been the newspaper's Environment Correspondent since 1986. He has won several awards, including one for Outstanding Work in Irish Journalism for a series of articles in 1979 entitled "Dublin - What Went Wrong?". He is the author of The Destruction of Dublin (Gill and Macmillan, 1985) and Saving the City (Tomar, 1989), two books that helped to change Irish public policy on urban renewal. More recently, he co-authored Ireland's Earthen Houses (A. A. Farmer, 1997) and edited The Ecological Footprint of Cities (International Institute for the Urban Environment,1997). His third book on Dublin, The Construction of Dublin (Gandon, 2000), became a non-fiction bestseller. He is also joint author with James Nix of Chaos at the Crossroads (Gandon, 2005), a book documenting the environmental destruction of Ireland. In October 2006, he was awarded an honorary DPhil by Dublin Institute of Technology.

Professor Kevin Murray is a chartered town planner and urbanist, and a Past President of the Royal Town Planning Institute. Educated at Aberdeen University and Oxford Brookes University, Kevin is a co-founder director and now Chair of The Academy of Urbanism. Beginning his career at the London Borough of Bromley, he joined Tibbalds

Partnership in 1985 and EDAW ten years later, before starting his own practice in 2002. He has been involved in development, regeneration and conservation projects all across the UK, many involving innovative leadership in placemaking, such as the award-winning 'place momentum' engagement process. He was co-author of the groundbreaking New Vision for Planning (RTPI, 2001) and also helped found the Urban Design Alliance (UDAL). He served on the Egan Task Group on Skills for Sustainable Communities and as a board member of the Academy for Sustainable Communities (ASC). An occasional media contributor on urbanism, Kevin was the focus of BBC Radio 4's 'Cities in 2010' and an adviser on Channel 4's award-winning 'Big Art' programme. He is Honorary Professor of Planning at Glasgow University.

Tony Reddy is an architect and urbanist. He was educated at University College Dublin and Trinity College Dublin. He was a Founding Director of The Academy of Urbanism, a co-founder and member of the Urban Forum, a member and former Chairman of the Housing and Sustainable Communities Committee (an RIAI / DoEHLG initiative) and a former President of the Royal Institute of Architects of Ireland. He is a Director of the Reddy Architecture and Urbanism Group, which is involved in architecture, urban design and urban regeneration projects in Ireland, the UK and throughout the European Union. His practice has completed masterplanning, urban design and architectural commissions including regeneration projects in towns and cities in Ireland, the United Kingdom and mainland Europe including Temple Bar West End, Custom House Square and Heuston South Quarter, Dublin, Cork Docklands and The Titanic Quarter, Belfast. His practice is currently designing town extensions and urban regeneration projects in Dublin, Belfast, Cork and Bucharest.

David Rudlin manages URBED (Urbanism Environment and Design). He is a planner by training and started his career with the city council in his home town of Manchester, working on the redevelopment of the Hulme estate. He was a founder member of the Homes for Change Housing Cooperative which built one of the flagship buildings in Hulme and co-wrote the Hulme Guide to Development. He joined URBED in 1990 to manage the Award-winning Little Germany project in Bradford. Since then he has managed a range of projects including Temple Quay 2 in Bristol, The New England Quarter in Brighton and the UK's fourth Millennium Village in Telford. He is the author of reports including '21st Century Homes' for the Joseph Rowntree Foundation, 'Tomorrow a peaceful path to urban reform' for Friends of the Earth and 'But would you live there?' for the Urban Task Force. This writing is summarised in *Sustainable Urban Neighbourhood* published by the Architectural Press and described by Richard Rogers as 'the best analysis (he) had read of the crisis facing the contemporary city'. David has been a member of the CABE Design Review Committee and a trustee of CUBE (the Centre for the Understanding of the Built Environment) in Manchester. He has been judge for the CNU awards in the US and the Europan Awards. He is an Academician of The Academy for Urbanism and is currently chair of the Sheffield Design Panel and BEAM in Wakefield.

David Taylor is a Senior Director at Alan Baxter and Associates. He leads the practice's work on master planning, urban design, transport and the public realm. He has a profound belief in the value that good design can bring to urbanism. His extensive experience includes major urban studies, city-scale master planning and regeneration projects, urban extensions, infill and new self-contained settlements. David is a key contributor to major public consultation events, and has led the authorship of a number of publications on urban design. He has a wealth of experience on a wide range of projects. His work for DCLG and CABE informed development policy in the Thames Gateway region and he has also been involved in the characterisation of settlement patterns in the Cambridge and Midlands areas. At

Ashford, David led the movement aspects of the Local Development Framework, aimed at handling the growth of the region from a population of 60,000 to 120,000 over the course of 25 years. This involved strategic work leading to the design of major infrastructure projects and the reworking of the Ashford ring road as an urban street.

John Thompson is the Founder-Chairman of The Academy of Urbanism, and Chairman of John Thompson and Partners, one of Europe's leading firms of Architects and Urbanists. In the 1980s he pioneered the use of Community Planning in the United Kingdom as a tool for engaging local people in the design of their neighbourhoods and has subsequently led a series of seminal projects that have simultaneously delivered physical, social and economic change. He was formerly chairman of the RIBA's Urbanism and Planning Group and a founding member of The Urban Villages Forum, and is currently a member of Yorkshire Forward's Urban and Rural Renaissance Panels. John has undertaken masterplanning and urban design projects in towns and cities throughout the UK and Europe. He is currently designing a series of new settlements in England, Scotland, Iceland, Moscow City Region and China.

Professor Frank Arneil Walker is an architect and formerly a professor at the University of Strathclyde, Glasgow. Frank Walker is one of Scotland's most distinguished architectural historians. His research has ranged from the national and Secession architectures of East-Central Europe to the development of urban form in Scotland. On these and other subjects, he has published widely in Britain and Europe. Amongst his books are several dealing with the architecture of Glasgow and the West of Scotland. He has a strong interest in the theory and practice of critical regionalism. He is Emeritus Professor of architecture at the University of Strathclyde. This text of this essay is based on papers first delivered in the 1990's and later published in Building Design (1995).

John Worthington is a Co-founder of DEGW, an International firm of strategic briefing and design consultants, a Director of The Academy of Urbanism, and chair of the Dublin City Urbanism advisory panel. His urban planning work includes envisioning for Birmingham City Centre (Highbury Initiative 1989–90); Stockley Park, Heathrow (1984–96); the Merchant City, Glasgow; city centre renewal, and high building strategies for Rotterdam, Dublin and London. Regeneration projects he has been responsible for include: The plan for the restructuring of the Carl Zeiss optics works in the centre of Jena, East Germany; Preparing the development brief and undertaking a city wide referendum for the Utrecht Central Station area, in the Netherlands. John is currently Deputy Chair of Cambridgeshire Horizons Quality panel; on the advisory groups of RIBA Building Futures, the Prince's Regeneration Trust and an advisor to Climate Change Capital's Property Investment Fund. He has also been a Board member of the London Thames Gateway Development Corporation (2004-09); Chair of CABE/RIBA Building Futures (2003-07) and CABE design panel. Academic appointments include Professor of Architecture and Director of the Institute of Advanced Architectural studies, The University of York (1992-97); Visiting Professor, Chalmers University of Technology, Gothenburg (2000-03); Graham Willis Professor, The University of Sheffield (2002-08) and Professorial Fellow at the University of Melbourne (2006-09). Since Co-founding DEGW in 1973, John has focussed on strategic briefing and supporting both the public and private sectors in making the most effective use of resources, by matching available space and buildings to organisational demand. Recent publications include Managing the Brief for Better Design (Routledge, Second Edition 2010) co-authored with Alastair Blyth, and Reinventing the Workplace (Architectural Press Second edition 2006).

CITIES

Amsterdam

Barcelona

Berlin

NEIGHBOURHOODS

Soho, London

Grainger Town, Newcastle

Temple Bar, Dublin

Brian Evans
& Frank McDonald

Introduction

This is the second anthology of place study published by the Academy. From the outset, the purpose of this series has been to document what we learn each year by studying finalists in the various categories of The Urbanism Awards. The Academy was established in the hope that we might re-learn and disseminate understanding and skills to make better places, streets, neighbourhoods, towns and cities. This is our pre-eminent mission.

As with Learning from Place 1, this book contains five chapters reviewing what we learned in the past year. This normative approach – with its emphasis on the assembly of evidence about urbanism – was introduced at the establishment of the awards process by the Academy as a means of getting to the heart of what makes a great city, a good neighbourhood, an interesting town or a vibrant street.

The essays on cities, towns, neighbourhoods, streets and places are produced by Academicians who participated in and usually led the assessments carried out by the Academy. These chapters are intended to be informed and readable, rather than academic or polemical. In some instances, they are idiosyncratic in the positions they take and the observations they make, reflecting each author's opinion on the issues of urbanism presented by the places under study. They follow broadly the criteria evaluated during the awards process such as governance, urban form and use, but they do so not in a strict or regimented manner – unlike the more structured evaluation of places compiled by the Academy for the purpose of voting on the Awards.

In his chapter on cities, Chris Balch faced the greatest challenge, to reflect on the three cities nominated for the European City of the Year Awards. To capture the essence of Berlin, Amsterdam and Barcelona in a short essay is a tall order, but Balch achieves a remarkable tour d'horizon by keeping it strategic and comparative.

By contrast, Brian Evans' task of dealing with the towns could not have been more straightforward. Kilkenny, Winchester and St. Andrews, each a small city in its own right, are quintessential examples of the market town, showing many aspects of their shared or distinctive character.

TOWNS

PLACES

Newcastle Quayside

St. Andrews

Kilkenny

Winchester

South Bank, London

The Peace and Winter Gardens, Sheffield

In his forensic examination of this year's neighbourhoods, David Rudlin explores the emerging phenomenon of the 'creative quarter' that is mapped onto central neighbourhoods in many British and Irish cities, by delving into Soho in London, Grainger Town in Newcastle and Temple Bar in Dublin.

Frank McDonald brings a reporter's eye to the public life inspired by this year's batch of great streets, with the text complemented by showing street typologies through sections and plans. And finally with places, David Taylor and Anthony Alexander continue Sarah Chaplin's categorisation of place as process and place as project begun in Learning from Place 1.

As editors for the series, we took the decision at the outset that the thematic study of place through city, town, neighbourhood, street and place should be juxtaposed with a contrasting theme to encourage reflection on the growing evidence base on the subject of urbanism.

This was begun in Learning from Place 1, with two chapters on the nature of space, place and life by Jonathan Meades and Frank McDonald – the former a polemic exploring what happens when things go awry, the latter a celebration of cities that work. In this volume we contrast the principal chapters with an inquiry into the theme of identity in urbanism – what this means and how people and places cope in a globalised world.

Robert Adam looks at identity and globalisation, John Worthington at identity and branding while Tony Reddy and Frank Walker attempt the impossible by trying to make explicit some key observations about regional identity in urbanism. In his introduction to a recent edition of the Architectural Review, Paul Finch wrote: "…the New Europe is beginning to revert to medieval groupings of areas that share economic or cultural interests, rather than necessarily the same language … regional planners in Brussels and Luxembourg have maps of Europe where national boundaries have evaporated, to be replaced by, for example, a region including Britain and Portugal because of proximity to the Atlantic".

We may detect a trace of irony here, yet the maps of the 'European Territory' published by the EU Commission make for interesting and informative study. Authors and commentators have mused on intercultural influences for centuries and there is ample evidence that travellers have brought back ideas or plunder, or both, from the places they visit that have influenced the way cities are built back home – for the best of them look no further than Italo Calvino's Invisible Cities.

STREETS

Regent Street, London

Buchanan Street, Glasgow

O'Connell Street, Dublin

Probably the first modern treatise on the phenomenon of globalisation was set out by Marshall McLuhan. It remains uncertain whether McLuhan ever actually penned the phrase 'the global village', but it seems beyond doubt that, at the very least, his enquiries and insights inspired the phrase that came to personify the world of television and later digital media.

In the first of our commissioned pieces, Robert Adam goes straight for the jugular – the phenomenon of globalisation as a trans-Atlantic, Christo-centric inspired hegemony driven by the wealth of the west and built by around 50 or so of the world's biggest or most celebrated architectural firms – with all but a few based in the USA and the UK.

In the second piece, John Worthington adopts a different tack: How do places project themselves and what is it that inspires cities to describe themselves in a 'soundbite' to create a brand in the urban prairie of the 21st century?

By contrast, regional expression in design is one of the thorniest challenges to get to grips with. Here's Finch again: "the architectural representation of regions is near-impossible, even if it were desirable, without resorting to the crudest of signs or signifiers of a historic past. What does Romansch architecture look like?"

But answering this question is precisely what Tony Reddy and Frank Walker attempt to do. In the process, Walker encapsulates the issue more succinctly than any other commentator known to us by proposing that the expression of identity in regional design involves the reconciliation of genius loci – the spirit of the place, with zeitgeist – the spirit of the times.

In the end, as Paul Finch also reflects, Sir Terry Farrell may well be right when he argues that the true client for any building is the place in which it sits and that the architectural response becomes not merely site-specific, but an absorption and reflection of cultural, economic and sociological influences.

And, so in our endpiece, Kevin Murray writes fluently and with great passion about the future course of the Academy. He sees and writes about its core values to go beyond the object to the processes that forge people and place. We might encapsulate his passion, shared by us all, in a paraphrase of Bill Shankley: Urbanism is not a matter of life and death – it's more important than that!

Prof. Chris Balch

Great cities don't just happen: they are made!

Amsterdam, Barcelona & Berlin

The life of great cities in Amsterdam (top), Barcelona (middle) and Berlin (bottom)

Amsterdam, Barcelona and Berlin - each of these great cities has delivered notable achievements in the field of urbanism. Study of the three cities by the Academy presents a major opportunity to document comparative experiences in successful place-making, to draw on experience from outside Britain and Ireland and to test conventional wisdom – to question whether or not there remain lessons to be learned in ways of delivering 'best practice' in city planning and development.

Amsterdam is a city that has a unique relationship with water. Occupying land which has been largely reclaimed from the shallows and estuaries of the North Sea, it is a city built on manmade space. The management and control of water determines urban plan and form even today as land reclamation continues and the city seeks to reconnect with the River Ij waterfront. This has produced a character and distinctiveness that is unmistakably Dutch with a strong emphasis on rigid street plans and architectural uniformity in a contemporary idiom. Within these constraints, individual expression can be muted but the result has a strong harmony and sense of purpose.

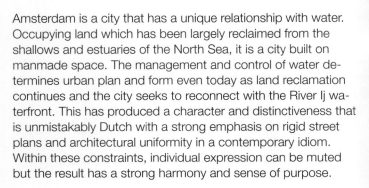

The intimacy of side streets in Barcelona (left) and Amsterdam (right)

Barcelona occupies a spectacular amphitheatre between ranges of Catalan mountains and the Mediterranean providing a powerful setting for a city with a strong and distinctive character. Its strong urban design is shaped by these constraints as well as the grid laid out by the Catalan urban planner Ildefons Cerdà in the 19th century. Barcelona is a city that offers a form of urban living that reflects its Mediterranean and Catalan heritage. Today, it virtually defines Mediterranean urbanism.

Sited on the River Spree on the North German plain, Berlin does not suffer from the physical limitations faced by Amsterdam and Barcelona. The making of Berlin is inextricably linked with the history of the German people. Standing at the interface between western and eastern Europe and now re-established as the capital of reunified Germany, Berlin has been the theatre in which the dialectic between political systems and approaches to urbanism and architecture has been played out. Today, it is a city of opportunities and optimism, reconnecting with its past while filling the empty spaces left by war and the Berlin Wall with buildings and spaces of the highest quality.

The achievements of all three cities demonstrate the importance of strong leadership both in their history and in their continued growth and development.

All, however, reflect their history and their role as centres of power and influence.

Amsterdam's evolution from small fishing settlement at the mouth of the Amstel to principal city of the Netherlands has been based on a strong tradition of collective organisation and planning. This was necessitated by the challenge of developing a city that critically depends on the control of water. The same merchants and aldermen who commissioned the art for which the city is renowned put in place building codes and plans to govern the orderly development of the city. The Plan of the Three Canals, approved in 1607, provided the framework for

View over Barcelona

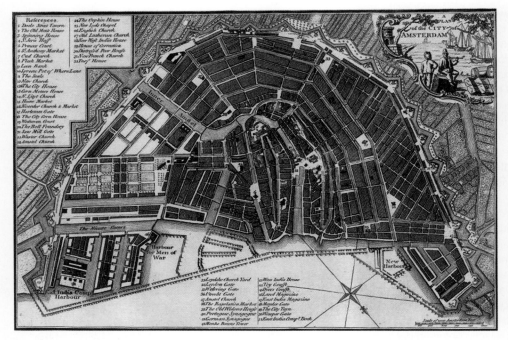

All three cities were planned, The Plan of the Three Canals in Amsterdam was approved in 1607

the development of historic Amsterdam and much of its subsequent growth. Today, Amsterdam is a well-managed city that builds on its long tradition of urban planning. The City Council uses its powers of planning and extensive land ownership (nearly 80% of the city is in the council's freehold ownership) to exercise considerable control over the way in which the city operates and develops.

Within the regional context of the Randstad, Amsterdam produces a new structure plan every 10 years that articulates a new vision for the city through increasing engagement of professionals, politicians and stakeholders. The Dutch tradition of rational planning also shows strong evidence of attempts to engage local communities. Following a period of centralisation in the late 20th century that produced the Bijlmermeer, an urban extension that has attracted much criticism, the city is now divided into 14 boroughs that have the responsibility for local delivery of neighbourhood and greenspace projects. Considerable efforts are made to work with local people. Indeed, there are deliberate efforts

made to harness the spirit and entrepreneurship of socially motivated groups. Amsterdam co-opts the energies of squatter and artistic communities to act as urban pioneers to help create interest in emerging locations and to use cultural activities to bring new life to the waterfront and regenerate former dockland areas. In this respect, Amsterdam combines a long established approach to urban development and management with a more radical edge. This is a city that seeks innovative solutions to the challenges it faces.

New townhouses in Amsterdam

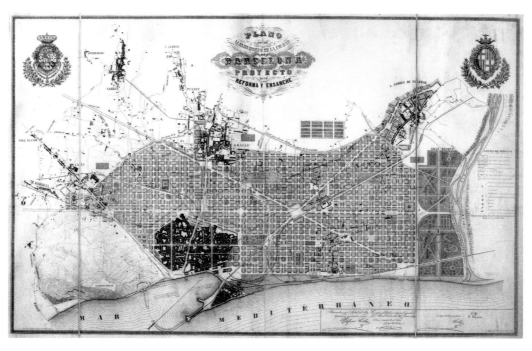

Cerdà's plan for Barcelona's New Town dates from the late 19th century

Barcelona's emergence as a major industrial and port city is inextricably linked with its role as the political and cultural heart of Catalonia. Civic leadership is closely aligned to provincial politics and the ongoing quest for a strong role and identity within Spain and Europe. The rivalry with Madrid is played out not just on the football field but in urban ambition forging strong civic leadership around a clear vision for Barcelona as the capital of Catalonia. This can be seen in the delivery of a series of transformational projects such as the 1992 Olympics, and the renewal of the former industrial waterfront. However, there is some evidence that the consensus which existed over an extended period may be breaking down in the face of strong development pressures. While recent changes in political control may have made Barcelona less outward looking, it remains a proud and well-run city.

The character of Barcelona today is underpinned by a strong physical planning framework. The heart of the historic city is surrounded by nine districts that are unified physically by the Cerdà plan for the Eixample laid out in the latter half of the 19th century. The Plan exerts a strong influence on urban form notwithstanding the underlying dramatic topography. While this form has been eroded to some degree by recent high-rise development, the determination of the city authorities to continue to deliver large-scale improvements is exemplified by the approach being pursued in the 22@ regeneration district - a new model of city providing a response to the challenges posed by the knowledge-based society. While there can be no

Parc de Diagonal Mar in Barcelona designed by Enric Miralles

Apartment blocks, Berlin

overland and inland water routes and the seat of power of the rulers of Brandenburg, Prussia and Germany. It was the Great Elector Frederick William and his successor Frederick, the first King of Prussia, who laid the foundations of the city which became the capital of the new German Empire in 1871. Developed on the basis of James Holbrecht's 19th Century plan for the imperial capital, Berlin grew rapidly and its fortunes became inextricably linked with the history of the German people.

The governance of Berlin poses unique challenges to the city and State. The remaking of a city that was physically and politically divided for almost half a century, and subject to radically different architectural and planning traditions, has been overwhelming. But the commitment shown in understanding these challenges and providing the resources to address the opportunities and needs is a story of outstanding achievement. The Senate of Berlin plays a leading role in establishing a clear masterplan for the historic core of the reunited city.

doubting the purposeful way in which the Barcelona city authorities have tackled improvements to the public realm, the degree to which local communities are actively involved is uncertain. Nonetheless, the results speak for themselves, for the quality of Barcelona's public realm has become a benchmark by which many cities judge themselves.

Berlin developed from a small settlement on the River Spree to become the centre of a network of

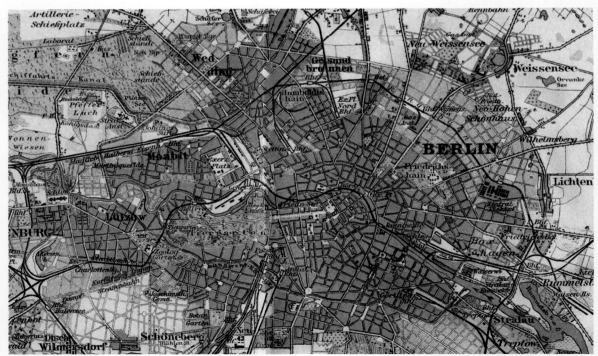

1894 Plan of Berlin

Berlin was transformed from a Medieval fortified city to the capital of an empire through James Holbrecht's 19th Century plan but has been equally shaped by the plans of the City Authority to unify its two halves following unification in 1989

The remnants of the Berlin Wall are a reminder of the past

This is based on 12 guiding principles and expressed as a model which is used as a tool for understanding the evolution of the urban plan and form, and guiding developers towards a recreation of James Holbrecht's original plan, often through design competitions.

As a city, Berlin has undergone and is undergoing a phenomenal process of change. From a war-ravaged place that was divided by political ideologies for decades, the city is successfully re-establishing itself as the capital of Germany with an economy based on public administration and service sector functions. The recreation of old meeting places such as Pariser Platz and Potsdamer Platz in old and new idioms bears testimony to the spirit of place, and Berliners and Germans are rightly proud of what has been achieved since reunification in 1990.

The Federal Government has undoubtedly had a major influence on the redevelopment of Berlin, particularly the new administrative quarter that includes the refurbished Reichstag and new Chancellery. But there is strong evidence of innovative approaches to engagement at community level, particularly in those parts of the city suffering from social disadvantage such as Kornerpark.

Barcelona figure ground plan

BARCELONA

Let me stand just here;
I'm framed by the evening light
In El Parc Güell.

The Spanish Village:
Show me how to dance, and then
Repeat it in stone.

City with wet feet,
Walking through the museum
And leaving timeprints.

The five elements:
Air, Earth, Fire, Water
And Barcelona.

If Barcelona
Was the only city left,
It would be enough.

I AMsterdam, a symbol of the pride that people have in the city

The three cities - Amsterdam, Barcelona and Berlin - demonstrate that there is no single approach to good city governance, but it is clear that bold leadership and a strong unifying vision are essential in contributing to successful city placemaking. Assessing a city's sense of place and distinctiveness needs to embrace both physical and cultural attributes. Some cities are recognisable by virtue of their iconic buildings and spaces whilst others simply exude an atmosphere that is unique. Amsterdam, Barcelona and Berlin must be reckoned amongst the more distinctive cities of Europe. Why?

The Dutch tradition of individualism within an ordered world is very much reflected in the physical form of development manifested in Amsterdam. Within the rigidity of an urban form determined by land reclamation, new ways are being sought to allow individual expression in building and design. Lessons have been learned from past mistakes and the resultant urban plan and form is unmistakably rational and Dutch with rectilinear street blocks and façades that directly abut the street, although the absence of defensible space at the front of buildings can give rise to starkness in new parts of the city.

In Amsterdam, buildings greatly influence the spaces between. This reflects the dominant role that engineers, architects and town planners play in the creation of the built environment. Superlative new public spaces are being created but these tend to be in parks rather than in urban squares and streetscapes. However, water space is key to the character of the city and adds substantially to its attractiveness as a place to live and to visit.

Barcelona is also a city with a long tradition of urban living that reflects its distinct Mediterranean and Catalan heritage, and gives great vibrancy to urban spaces. This is a city that generates a strong and justifiable local pride of place. The streets, squares, parks and walkways are animated by day and night by social activity adding huge vibrancy to city life.

Barcelona has successfully become a place for people of all ages

Amsterdam street life mixes cycles, pedestrians and cars

From the historic core across its wider city blocks, Barcelona delivers a great sense of place and belonging. This is reinforced by the high density of the built form and the distinctive character of the city's architecture personified by the work of Antoni Gaudí. People feel great pride in their city which is well cared for and well used.

The rigid grid plan imposes a uniformity that contrasts sharply with the surrounding hills and the Mediterranean shore. Within this framework, there is a strong pattern of streets and squares that define local character. The two main exceptions to this are the historic city core that exhibits a more organic form and the emerging 22@ district that incorporates new architectural forms, which represent a departure from the traditional pattern of urbanism in Barcelona.

The city is an exemplar of how to achieve active street frontages. The high density of the urban blocks – typically 7 or 8 storeys – generates substantial street-level activity along generously proportioned boulevards, reaching a pinnacle on the commercial Diagonal and the world-famous Las Ramblas. This is a dense city with formal parks such as Park Güell (originally the centrepiece for a speculative housing development by Count Güell

Quality public space in Berlin

– Gaudí's patron) as well as informal areas such as Montjuic which accommodated the 1992 Olympics. Informality takes place in the streets and squares, and along the coast, land has been reclaimed from industry to create a great seaside promenade stretching for several kilometres.

Berlin is recreating its historic spaces and places, many blighted by the impact of the Wall. The mending of the urban fabric involving the renaissance of great streets such as Unter Den Linden and Friedrichstrasse, and the reconnection of people with generous green spaces and the River Spree and canal waterfronts is creating a city with immense style and appeal. The memory of place remains strong in Berlin despite a 50-year hiatus. The remaking of places such as Pariser Platz and Potsdamer Platz reflects the original plans swept away during and

Gràcia in Barcelona being prepared for the annual festival (left) and an avenue in Berlin (above)

after the war but they have been reinterpreted in a modern or neo-classical idiom. Their success, measured by the intensity of use, points to the validity of this approach. The creation of walkways along the Spree, the pedestrianisation of major public spaces and the generous scale of the city's streets makes Berlin a great place to walk. The redevelopment of historic streets such as Friedrichstrasse is incorporating active frontages, although much retail activity has been lost to suburban and out-of-town development. The intensity of pedestrian and cycle activity and the medium to high density of the city's residential districts promotes a sense of security and self-surveillance; this is not a city that relies on CCTV.

Berlin possesses superlative open spaces such as the Tiergarten and is crisscrossed with watercourses and lakes that support abundant wildlife. In some areas, open spaces work much less well and the management of local green areas is sometimes poor, but the overriding impression is of a good balance between built form and the natural environment.

In their different ways, Amsterdam, Barcelona and Berlin achieve a rich sense of place strongly related to their urban form and context: Amsterdam – the waterfront city with a distinctive urban form imposed by the management of water and the need to impose uniformity; Barcelona – the dense Mediterranean city whose expansion has taken place around a regular urban grid; Berlin – the reunified German Capital incorporating great boulevards and squares and generous water and green spaces. Interwoven with this physical form is a strong and distinctive cultural heritage that expresses itself in the richness of design and urban living for which all three cities are renowned. Safeguarding distinctiveness and quality in the face of pressures to maintain international competitiveness and accommodate growing populations represents a major challenge for European cites. Amsterdam, Barcelona and Berlin are all actively engaged in regenerating old city districts and creating new ones. Their success in

Amsterdam embraces contemporary architecture whether it be in modern office buildings or town houses (below)

achieving this is both a measure of their ability to adapt to changing demands and the extent of their commitment to maintaining continuity.

As well as a key commercial centre in the Netherlands, Amsterdam is seeking to position itself as a competitive location for international business. This may be seen in the regeneration of the Ij waterfront and the creation of new business districts such as

Amsterdam figure ground plan

AMSTERDAM

City built on water, city built on bikes
Bikes flowing like water crossing the road
When you least expect 'em!

City built on commerce, city built on art
Bikes rushing like paintings across your eyes
And the water reflects 'em!

Just walk beside this canal with an ear open for bells
And the constant hum of Amsterdam
Like the sound of the waves in an ear-clamped shell:
Barge-splash, taxi horn, gallery-door-slam.

City built on grids, city built on squares,
Bike as metaphor for the questing mind:
Grab some ideas and pedal 'em!

New office development in Berlin

Zuidas that aim to offer an attractive business environment with superb transport connections. This strategy for growth is being actively promoted by the city council working in partnership with private sector developers and investors.

Amsterdam has embarked on a major development programme aimed at accommodating population and employment growth. Family housing is being built in both new and regenerating neighbourhoods and efforts are being made to attract and retain higher income groups through providing more tenure choice.

The challenge of providing economic opportunities for all are clearly recognised and are reflected in working with economically and socially marginalised sections of society. This includes working with squatter and self help groups as well as racial minorities. Innovative approaches are being developed to tackle 'hard to reach' groups enabling them to build selfconfidence and participate in the

undoubted opportunities being created within the city's market-orientated economy.

The pro-active approach of the city council is guiding new investment towards disadvantaged communities and major regeneration and development locations. Investment in infrastructure is leading the way in opening up these areas, supported by a strong design framework. Examples include the Ijburg self-build housing and the user-led design in Bijlmermeer. High quality design in public buildings is also a feature of the regeneration plans focused around the new public library.

Barcelona is thriving and remains Spain's principal commercial city with a well-balanced economic base. In addition to employment focused in the core of the city, new business districts are being developed on the periphery with good access to road and air connections. The city will shortly benefit from improved high speed train connections. However, it is unclear the extent to which all sections of society

The Ramblas running through the heart of Barcelona Old Town

are benefiting from the economic and development growth of the city. There remain significant concentrations of poorer social housing and evidence of poverty amongst immigrant communities. But for those who can afford to live in the city, opportunities abound.

Berlin is a city of opportunity for commercial investment and enterprise. Led by the public sector and guided by a strong planning framework, the city continues to attract private developers and investors who are contributing to the creation of a dynamic urban environment. Alongside large-scale corporate investment, there is a rich mix of individual entrepreneurship reflected in small to medium-sized creative businesses as well as innovative meanwhile uses.

The regeneration of Berlin has been driven by the decision of the Federal Government to re-establish the city as the capital of Germany. This has led to extraordinary levels of investment. Major employers are now establishing their headquarters in the city although Berlin faces strong competition from established commercial centres such as Hamburg, Frankfurt and Munich. Smaller scale enterprises are thriving based on the creativity of the city's population.

The reunification of the city has posed major challenges in bringing together two different economic systems. Traditional manufacturing employment has largely disappeared leaving a major challenge to find replacement jobs and re-skill the workforce. The city is pursuing active programmes to ensure that as far as possible, the new opportunities being created reach all sectors and areas.

Icaria Avenue in Barcelona: Steel trees designed by Carme Pinós and Enric Miralles to provide shade in a street where an underground sewer made tree planting impossible

The city is providing leadership to the private sector through its pro-active approach to planning and its investment in infrastructure and the public realm. This is demonstrated in one project where individuals have been given the opportunity to create high-quality self build houses in the heart of the city. Elsewhere, the public sector takes a leading role in stimulating projects such as the Potsdamer Platz quarter through development and design competitions. Employment in knowledge-based and creative industries is also being promoted with a focus on attracting young people to Berlin.

Potsdamer Platz, Berlin

New family housing, Amsterdam

The authorities are making strenuous efforts to encourage people to live in the inner city. New family housing is being provided and historic housing areas are being restored and renewed. Much needs to be done to address the legacy of poor quality housing in the former east.

For all three cities, the challenge is to accommodate growth and attract investment in a manner that respects their unique character and sense of place. At Zuidas, the City of Amsterdam is seeking to create an international business district that has a distinctively Dutch sense of place; in Barcelona, there has been a significant departure from the conventional block form which has served the city so well with the emergence of high-rise development; for Berlin, the need to rebuild large swathes of the city centre has provided the opportunity to recreate historic places. The key to success may lie in the existence of a clear plan for the city and a determination to remain true to that vision.

Increasingly, cities need to respond to a sustainability agenda, requiring a balancing of economic needs against environmental and social considerations. For each city, this poses different challenges and has evoked differing responses. Amsterdam exists despite its environment. The city's history has been one of controlling nature rather than living in harmony with it. Reclamation continues today giving rise to conflict with the marine environment. However, experimental solutions are being developed to reduce dependence on engineered flood defences by 'building' on the water. Strenuous efforts are being made to redevelop former port and port-related industrial areas with a new mix of uses. The city contains many examples of the innovative reuse of buildings including shipyard sheds, gasworks and offices, some involving cultural activities. As a compact city, Amsterdam contains a good balance and mix of uses from the historic city core to its residential neighbourhoods. It has a well developed street plan that reflects the way in which land has been progressively reclaimed to accommodate growth. This helps to define a series of blocks and neighbourhoods within which public and commercial facilities are provided. The need to conserve the historic fabric at the core of the city has resulted in the decentralisation of some facilities to the ring road, although civic and cultural provision remains concentrated in the city centre. Amsterdam has also maintained a balance between investment in public transport and road infrastructure. As a result, the city is very well served by a variety of transport modes. However, most notable is the extensive use of the bicycle as a practical means of transport. Provision for the bicycle is incorporated into new developments and its presence is ubiquitous – a significant contribution to a sustainable lifestyle.

The city faces a substantial challenge in seeking to accommodate more housing for the people who want to live in

Amsterdam has led the way in promoting cycling

Berlin figure ground plan

BERLIN

Can you take me to the heart of the city ?
Ah, I see; the heart is everywhere.
Can you direct me to the main railway station ?
Oh: I will recognise it by the beauty and the sound.
I want to experience history and philosophy,
I understand. If I just sit it will come to me.
Could you direct me to an experience that will make me gasp ?
Oh: I must wait until nightfall and open my ears and eyes.
Can you tell me what makes the city move and breathe ?
Ah, I see; I must stand close to the buildings and hear the bloodbeat.

The Sony Centre and Bahn Tower in Potsdamer Platz

Street life in Barcelona

Amsterdam. Particular efforts are being made to attract and retain families by providing more opportunities for owner occupation. That said, the city recognises the need to make special efforts to provide opportunities for disadvantaged communities and has developed innovative approaches to engaging with marginalised groups. It is a city that cares for people.

The Dutch approach to urban planning and architecture appears to place more emphasis on infrastructure and buildings than upon the public realm, although there is significant investment taking place in creating and regenerating green spaces. Westerpark provides an example of an impressive new urban park on the site of a former gasworks. Elsewhere, contaminated land at Ijburg has been converted to green space. The city's open spaces are under tremendous pressure of use and require constant reinvestment and maintenance. Within the historic core of the city, there is a vibrant pattern and mix of uses. This is less evident in the new development areas, perhaps as a result of lower densities

and the absence of strong street blocks. In certain parts of the suburbs, modernist approaches to housing have undermined this pattern but efforts are being made to rectify the resultant social problems. After the planning mistakes of the early 1970s that led to the creation of segregated communities on the periphery of the city, new developments such as Ijburg seek to achieve well-balanced neighbourhoods through the provision of a mix of house type and tenure.

In Barcelona, the rapid growth of the city region is placing considerable strains on the natural resources of land and water and, apart from prominent solar power arrays, there is little evidence that Barcelona is pursuing a strategy aimed at reducing dependency on carbon-based products. Much new development depends in both form and location upon the use of the car and is increasingly making use of non-traditional materials.

Efforts continue to regenerate former port and industrial areas of the city although this is matched by new development on the edge of the city offering good access to motorway and air services. As a result, car usage continues to grow although Barcelona offers residents and visitors a well-developed rapid transit system. New development areas are supported by investment in public transport and some efforts are being made to ration road space in the city centre. However, provision continues to be made for the car and the location of new commercial activities reflects access to road transport.

Cerdà's plan ensures that Barcelona has a coherent and interconnected street network that serves to define city blocks and neighbourhoods and supports a clear hierarchy of functions. While this is breaking down to some extent as a result of the development of shopping malls in suburban locations, the city centre remains the dominant location for commercial activities. The mixed nature of Barcelona's economy and neighbourhoods provides its inhabitants with a range of housing and employment opportunities. While there is evidence of segregation, the city's lifestyle encourages communal activity and a good degree of social harmony. In this regard, it is a well functioning city that is easy to 'read'.

Barcelona is a user-friendly city as judged by the number of people that live and work there and visit for leisure, cultural and sporting purposes. To some degree, the city is the victim of its own success with rapidly rising property prices pushing young people out to surrounding areas. But within the city itself no one can doubt the rich and enticing nature of the urban fabric. Barcelona remains a highly civilised place to live and to visit. However, the sheer number of people on the streets has also attracted a criminal element that means that people have to be on their guard. This is particularly the case in the narrow streets and alleys of the old city and may reflect the marginalisation of some sections of society.

Lying on the North German plain, Berlin has taken advantage of the land and water space it occupies to create an urban environment in harmony with its surroundings. Surrounded by windfarms and pursuing active measures to reduce and recycle waste, Berlin is trying to minimise its use of non-renewable resources although, with brick and wood as the locally available building materials, it is perhaps surprising to see so much use of steel and glass in the modern Berlin.

The 'Whale' apartment block in Amsterdam

Berlin is fortunate in having a strong public transport network around which to build a unified functioning city. This has led to the rediscovery of the historic core supporting higher order functions linked to strong neighbourhoods that support a range and mix of uses. The return to James Holbrecht's plan based on major urban blocks capable of supporting a mix of residential and employment uses is encouraging the re-emergence of the street block as the dominant urban form. Its public transport system, including S-Bahn, U-Bahn, trams, and buses, is excellent. In addition, there is excellent provision for cyclists and pedestrians linking all parts of the city. Although heavily subsidised, public transport supports a well functioning city with capacity for further growth. Berlin is a city that works.

With high levels of public transport usage and a green setting, Berlin is striving for a more environmentally sustainable form of urban development. Achieving social sustainability across a city divided on social, economic and political lines has posed a huge challenge that the city is seeking to match through innovative renewal programmes focusing on both social and physical needs. The journey from a wall-divided city to the open Berlin that exists today has been simply extraordinary.

There is a clear distinction between the northern European cities of Amsterdam and Berlin and Barcelona as a Mediterranean city with very different physical contexts and environmental demands. While this inevitably leads to some difference of approach, all three cities have invested in well developed public transport systems and are seeking to promote sustainable forms of urban living. This depends to a significant degree upon the development of functioning neighbourhoods which contain a mix of uses and housing types and tenures, and a strong city centre containing higher order functions.

Underlying each of the three cities lies a strong unifying plan that persists today and imposes a framework within which development and renewal can take place. The genius of the Plan of the 3 Canals, of Cerdà and Holbrecht continues to exert an influence today demonstrating that great cities don't just happen – they are made using enduring principles of urbanism.

Converted pump house on the River Spree in Berlin

Robert Adam

The Globalisation of Place

While good urbanism promotes the unique identity of place, we will all be aware of a contrary direction. In architecture and urbanism, there are ideas and an aesthetic that cross borders, applied by international or local firms seeking to be international. It is not only architectural and urban design practices that promote a unified modern and western model for the creation of place but, such is the status of this internationalism, it is also being championed by cities that seek to promote themselves as 'global'. This powerful force in the creation of new places and the modification of old places cannot be ignored. There is little to be gained in railing against it without trying to understand what is driving it and what forces will assist us in seeking 'to enhance local character' and express 'the culture or cultures of … places'.

This internationalism, or more properly, transnationalism, is generally called 'globalisation'. Globalisation represents the spread of a homogenised culture and the consequent erosion of national and local character. At first sight, it would seem that globalisation and responding to the traditions of the place are running in wholly contrary directions and on a collision course. While there is some truth in this, it may not be the whole story. To understand why, we have to try and understand globalisation – not an easy task with a work in progress.

Any discussion of the modern condition anywhere in the world must include a discussion of globalisation. As Martin Albrow, tells us: "Globalisation is the most significant development and theme in contemporary life and social theory to emerge since the collapse of Marxist systems[1]."

So what is globalisation?

The movement of people and expansion of trade has been taking place for millennia. But globalisation as a term seems to have originated – quite symbolically as it turns out – in an American Express advertising campaign in the mid-1970s[2]. It was a phenomenon waiting for a catchword and, once coined, the word spread quickly to sum up what has become, according to Anthony Giddens: "the intensification of worldwide social relations in such a way that local happenings are shaped by events occurring many miles away and vice versa."[3]

This 'intensification of worldwide social relations' has many facets that can be individually important. They are listed by the German social philosopher Jürgen Habermas: "By 'globalisation' is meant the cumulative processes of a worldwide expansion of trade and production, commodity and financial markets, fashions, the media and computer programs, news and communications networks, transportation systems and flows of migration, the risks engendered by large-scale technology, environmental damage and epidemics, as well as organised crime and terrorism."[4] A formidable list.

The key initiating events of this process, again significantly, took place in the middle of the last century under American tutelage. These were: the Bretton-Woods Agreement of 1944 which led (eventually) to the creation of the World Bank and the International Monetary Fund; the Atlantic Charter of 1941 between Britain and the United States which led to the creation of the United Nations in 1945 and the Universal Declaration of Human Rights in 1948.

The Bretton-Woods Agreement set up a global system for regulating international trade based on the United States and European free-market system. The origins of the United Nations lay in the Atlantic Charter of 1941 between Britain and the US that set out the moral position of the Allied Powers. After the war, the United Nations took up these principles and attempted to establish a system for the avoidance of inter-state conflict. The subsequent Universal Declaration of Human Rights put in place an Anglo-Saxon concept of the right of individuals over and above their community, nation or state. All four events significantly modified the nation-state system that was created in Europe by the Treaties of Westphalia in 1648, which gave states - and only states - both the right to wage war and absolute rights over the lives of their citizens.

The advancement of transnational human rights was stalled by the Cold War. The record of the UN has been disappointing and its authority has been further undermined by the US in the lead-up to the Iraq war. Outside communist control, however, the internationalisation of free trade and the establishment of an accelerating series of international treaty organisations have, from the beginning, led to a successful capitalist global free-market economic system and a corresponding growth of global industries. So successful, in fact, that non-communist states have had to adapt to global industry, rather than the other way round. Indeed, the structural strength of

Amsterdam

the free-market global economy contributed to the collapse of the Soviet Empire in 1989 and the free-market has now been adopted not only by Russia, but by India and China in the early 1990s.

Leading the way in the new global economy were North Atlantic and primarily American corporations. These were the inheritors of the Enlightenment, a unique combination of rationalist and scientific philosophies in eighteenth-century Europe, the Industrial Revolution and free-market system in Britain, and the libertarianism of the American Revolution. These collectively came to be called simply 'modernity'. At first, this led to the domination and colonisation of much of the non-industrialised world, primarily by Britain. American domination of the so-called 'developed' world after the Second World War led to decolonisation and the creation of a US-dominated global economic system. This is what we have today except that, as might be expected in a truly free global system, the nationality of the corporations becomes less and less relevant. Nevertheless, the global economic culture continues to be based on the transatlantic model.

This model is based on the Enlightenment principle that, as Baron d'Holbach said in 1753, 'reasonable opinions' must take over and 'the vain chimeras of men' must be removed – 'inconceivable theology, ridiculous fables, impenetrable mysteries, [and] puerile ceremonies', in other words cultural traditions. Reason would allow mankind to rise above the irrational differences created by cultures and unify as liberal individuals to bring progress to an ever-improving world. Progress would involve change and change would be driven by continual experiment. In the US, these principles when combined with the liberty of every individual both to innovate and consume, created a highly successful and expanding industrial and capitalist market system.

Once American wealth had overtaken Britain and the other European powers, the US managed a progressive expansion of its economy by forcing decolonisation on the bankrupt European powers they supported and then by the effective imposition of its free-market system on the rest of the world. American market expansion, however, brought with it a political system that linked the freedom of markets with its own concept of political freedom.

As early as 1904 Hugo Munsterburg wrote that "the duty of America is to extend its political system to every quarter of the globe: other nations will thus be rated according to their ripeness for this system, and the history of the world appear one long and happy education of the human race up to the plane of American conception."[5] Prophetic words.

The early start of the US and its North Atlantic satellites in the global arena allowed industrial brands from these countries to dominate the global marketplace. Brands such as Coca Cola, McDonalds, Nike and Starbucks have become symbols of globalisation. In the words of Theodore Levitt in the Harvard Business Review in 1983, 'everywhere everything gets more and more like everything else as the world's preference structure is relentlessly homogenised.'

This principle extends to the built environment.

In the early twentieth century in Europe and then in the US an architectural style emerged that drew its inspiration from the principles of the Enlightenment. This style, modernism, made an aesthetic out of the symbolic representation of rationality, and innovation. The principles of modernism were considered to be universal and beyond the historicism of culture. It almost completely took over the architectural and planning professions just after the founding events of globalisation.

Modernism has joined with other global brands to represent the success of the global free market. Much as the North Atlantic economic system came to dominate global markets, the Modernist association with the principal building types identified with globalisation – the corporate office, the airport, the international hotel and the shopping mall – provide a clear symbolic link with the engines of global capital expansion. In a very short space of time, the homogenisation of global consumerism had its parallel in the homogenisation of city centres throughout the world. The glass-walled office block had become the Coca-Cola of architecture. Now, without reference to signage or vehicle registration plates, it is often impossible to identify the global location of parts of San Francisco, Osaka, Saõ Paolo, Brussels, Berlin and Shanghai. The North Atlantic type has become globally dominant. The most telling evidence of this is the nationality of the 55 global architectural firms - firms with fully-functioning offices in other global regions. Of these, 80% have their head offices in English-speaking countries and even the two Hong Kong firms on the list were founded in the nineteenth-century colonial period by UK expatriates.

Globalised commercial architecture has developed a symbiotic relationship with a new breed of global star architects. As cities now compete to attract global investment and tourism, they seek 'brand differentiation' and symbolic modernity. The commissioning of public buildings by star architects is now an established marketing technique. The buildings must be (in the literal sense of the word) extra-ordinary and designed by one of a small band of global architects whose nationality is not significant. The names are familiar and include Frank Gehry, Daniel Libeskind, Jean Nouvel, Rem Koolhaas, Norman Foster, Santiago Calatrava and Renzo Piano. The personal status of these architects is now so great and the demand for their presence so high, that their work is almost by necessity strongly conceptual and cannot rely on any detailed study of fine grain or culture of the locality. Indeed, as it is the intention that the building should be an iconic global product, local distinctiveness is often not a desirable characteristic.

Urban design has run a parallel course. Global commercial firms and star architects have joined in the unregulated growth industry of masterplanning. A universal type of 'big box and boulevard' masterplan has evolved. This consists of orthogonal or non-orthogonal grids of wide streets or boulevards which offer the maximum opportunities for showing off large 'iconic' buildings.

Agbar Tower, Barcelona by the French Architect Jean Nouvel

The Forum Building in Barcelona by the Swiss architects Herzog & de Meuron

Of even more concern than this, architects such as Zaha Hadid have taken their deracinated conceptual design techniques into urbanism and it can only be their star reputation that makes anyone take their computerised diagrams seriously.

While most commentators agreed that globalisation will not be reversed without a major physical catastrophe, they also agree that the phenomenon is more complex than the simple flattening out of world culture. There is a reverse side to homogenisation and that is *localisation*.

Now that the successful economies of states come to depend on attracting free-floating global commerce, as the sociologist Daniel Bell famously put it in the 1980s, "the nation-state has become too small to solve global problems and too large to deal with local ones". But nation-states and national identity are largely nineteenth-and twentieth-century inventions that attempted to homogenise varied communities within their borders. In diminishing the role of the nation-state, globalisation has lifted the lid on local culture and identities. As Jan Aart Scholte points out, "when faced with a seemingly vast, intangible and uncontrollable globality, many people have turned away from the state to their local 'home' in hopes of enhancing their possibilities of community and self determination."[6] Indeed, in 1991, Larry Chartand identified over 5,000 discrete communities of peoples - or nations - amongst only 200 states.[7]

Regionalisation and the re-emergence of micro-nations is a worldwide phenomenon. Examples among a great many include decentralisation in Argentina, the legal primacy of the Catalan language in the Catalan region of Spain, the independence of the central Asian states from the Russian empire, and the 74th Amendment of the Indian constitution - to say nothing of the resurgence of Welsh and Scots and Irish Gaelic. The instruments of global communication - television and the internet - are used to reinforce the identity of re-emerging nations. Satellite broadcasts have assisted the survival of the Inuktituk language; the Cree Indians and the European Arctic-circle Sami both have own-language-entry web sites that act as a community focus.

And yet, globalisation is based on the power of reason and acceptance of change brought in by the Enlightenment as a contrary to the conservatism of, what are called, 'traditional societies'. This enquiring, scientific, rational and liberal outlook continues to be the engine of expanding globalisation. Is this not a paradox? Where then do the traditions and symbols of local culture, the old enemy of unrestrained progress, fit into this new world?

So successful has been the rational global system that there are very few simply traditional cultures left. A society that can rely on tradition as the sole justification for its actions without recourse to any logical reasoning is extremely rare. As Anthony Giddens says, "The end of tradition doesn't mean that tradition disappears, as the Enlightenment thinkers wanted. On the contrary, it continues to flourish everywhere. But less and less … is it tradition lived in the traditional way."[8] The last bastion of this level of tradition in any wider social context is religious doctrine, which is either left well alone in any rational debate or takes the extreme form of fundamentalism. Otherwise, wholly traditional cultures are so rare that any such group would now have its culture carefully protected as an ethnic relic.

Traditional culture is no longer the enemy of reason and progress. Almost everywhere, traditions are discretionary or life-style choices – there's always an alternative. To quote Giddens again, "traditions only persist in so far as they are made available to discursive justification and are prepared to enter into open dialogue not only with other traditions but with alternative modes of doing things."[9]

Cultures, their traditions, their symbols and their role in social cohesion are a key component in the complex world of the new globality. They are not the self-justifying traditions of the past but rational or reflexive traditions, open to self-criticism, modernity and development.

We can and must now examine cultural traditions for what they are worth. We can find things that we cannot support: female circumcision, forced child labour or the suppression of minorities. And we can find a great deal that is of value: a sense of place in a world, the cohesion of a community and settlement of individuals within it, a deposit of accumulated empirical knowledge, or an established methodology for the use of low energy resources.

The physical manifestation of localisation is a concern with the identity of place. In the last fifteen years there has been a growing urbanist movement specifically concerned with the individuality and identity of place. One of the earliest and the most successful is the American Congress for the New Urbanism (CNU), which was founded in 1993 and seeks 'the reconfiguration of sprawling suburbs into communities of real neighbourhoods and diverse districts' and 'the redevelopment of towns and cities [to] respect historical patterns, precedents and boundaries.[10]' A Vision of Europe was founded a year previously in Bologna with the objective of 'the creation of villages, neighbourhoods, cities and even metropolises, marked by new structural and formal qualities that will make them comparable to their historic counterparts.[11]' In 2001 the International Network for Traditional Building, Architecture and Urbanism (INTBAU) was founded with a statement that 'local, regional and national traditions provide the opportunity for communities to retain their individuality with the advance of globalisation'. Three years later, a sister organisation to the CNU, the Council for European Urbanism (CEU), was established in Bruges and promotes 'the distinctive character of European cities, towns, villages and countryside [and] consolidation, renewal and growth in keeping with regional identity and the aspirations of citizens[12]'. Most recently, The Academy of Urbanism was created in 2006 out of an initiative by the then president of the RIBA, George Ferguson, and asserts that "the design of spaces and buildings should be influenced by their context and seek to enhance local character and heritage."

This direction in urbanism is based on the realisations that, for all its apparent rationality, 'big-box-and-boulevard' urbanism does not deliver a successful urban environment. The continuity of cultural identity in urban design is adopted not just because it is traditional but because its value is recognised for its own sake. This is a model case of reflexive tradition. The fact that tradition delivers community identity and incorporates the accumulated experience of previous generations is recognised, not as a romantic intention to return to the past, but as a modern and reasoned approach to the present. It is now clear that traditional urban form was itself a sophisticated response to climate, resources and local conditions gained over time. Furthermore, traditional cities have a symbiotic relationship with the communities that occupy them: the form has developed around the way of life of the people and the people identify with the form. This is not rebuilding the past; it is providing the best conditions for the future and can incorporate whatever technological advances are appropriate.

Now that we can understand the relationship between the global and local, between homogenisation and localisation, we can see that urbanism itself is a part of the complex new conditions created by globalisation. As we turn outwards to an ever more connected world, we are also able to turn inwards to community and locality. Not only are we able to connect with our cultural traditions, in a globalised world, it is essential that we do so.

Peter Calthorpe - Part of the New Urbanism movement in the US

1. The Global Age, Polity Press, 1996, [p98-90]
2. Ronald Niezen, A World Beyond Difference, Blackwell, 2004, [p47]
3. The Consequences of Modernity, Polity Press, 1991, [p64]
4. The Divided West, Polity Press, 2006, [p175]
5. The Americans, McLure Phillips, [p6]
6. Globalisation: a critical introduction, Palgrave Macmillan, 2005 [p189-90]
7. A New Solidarity among Native Peoples, World Press Review
8. Runaway World, Profile Books, 2002 (2nd edn) [p43]
9. Ulrich Beck, Anthony Giddens, Scott Lash, Reflexive Modernization: Politics, Tradition and Aesthetics in the Modern Social Order, Polity Press, 1994, [p105]
10. CNU Charter and Principles Point 6
11. Vision of Europe, Charter of the City of the New Renaissance, Point 2
12. The Charter for European Urbanism, Stockholm, 6 November 2003, 'Action'

Brian Evans
& Chris Brett

Great Towns, Small Cities

Kilkenny, St. Andrews & Winchester

Kilkenny (top), St. Andrews (middle) and Winchester (bottom)

The towns of Winchester, St. Andrews and Kilkenny are notable for their similarities and for their contrasts: all are ancient and all are small cities, whether formally or informally. But all three are quite different to one another. One is English, one Irish and one Scottish, each therefore with its own racteristics and qualities of governance, geography and culture.

All three enjoy good governance. Winchester is home to a county and a city authority. The city supports an intelligent and articulate community with pockets of relative deprivation and a small ethnic community. Collaboration between the City Council and Winchester Area Community Action (one of a number of partnerships) seeks to 'reach out to ... minority and excluded groups to make the town a more inclusive place'. There is clear evidence of a collective vision set out in Winchester – Towards our Future, drawn up by the Town Forum and the City Council encourages community associations to prepare neighbourhood plans and participate in local networks and amenity groups. A local architects panel contributes aesthetic advice to the planning authority.

Winchester, therefore, has adopted an inclusive approach to the issues it faces. The process of regeneration of the town is being managed carefully and a series of sensitive masterplanning exercises have been promoted, for example, major consultation exercises

have been undertaken for the regeneration project at Silver Hill. The City Council has an open-minded approach to local stakeholder and community engagement and promotes participation in decision-making, particularly in respect of the city's future.

By contrast, the governance of St. Andrews is improving rapidly following many years when decision-making was perceived as remote from the town and from local people. Now, the public agencies, major institutions - such as the University - and civic and community groups have signed up to the collective St. Andrews World Class Vision, which promotes a well managed town to meet the needs of local residents, businesses and the student and visitor community. After decades of under-investment in public space, the period since 2004 has seen major investments in infrastructure, streetscape and design with an emphasis on high-quality materials and craftsmanship, befitting the town's international profile. A robust and thorough community and business consultation process, although somewhat prolonged, has been put in place in advance of the construction of new public realm works. Published Design Guidelines have been formally adopted for new development, alterations to streetscape and all buildings including shop fronts.

There remains a widely-held local view that St. Andrews is overlooked for public investment, with resources being diverted to other parts of Fife that have more pressing socio-economic needs. However, political change in May 2007 resulted in greater decentralisation of decision-making and a more positive response to locally informed decisions. Extensive consultation in the preparation of the new St. Andrews and East Fife Local Plan has been well-received with 'drop in' sessions, street surveys, public meetings and written feedback leading to a commendation at the Scottish Awards for Quality in Planning.

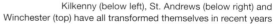

Kilkenny (below left), St. Andrews (below right) and Winchester (top) have all transformed themselves in recent years

Views of Kilkenny left and right including the arts festival (centre)

Kilkenny

Kilkenny has endured through the centuries by adapting to the needs of its inhabitants, whilst retaining its unique appeal to visitors. The unique built heritage and winding streetscapes provides a link to ancient times whilst continuing to be a vibrant place to live and work. Kilkenny retains its charm by allowing modern uses in old buildings so that they don't become ossified or neglected. The enjoyment of old buildings with modern uses such as the Shee Alms House has been an important policy for the City Authority. In 2007, Kilkenny celebrated 800 years of town government and the following year the town marked 400 years as a city since the 1609 Charter conferred by James I.

The Kilkenny City and Environs Development Plan represents the output to an inclusive exercise involving the public, developers, planners and elected members. One of the main aims of the plan is to achieve the 'ten minute city' to ensure that citizens and residents of Kilkenny do not have to travel more than ten minutes from their homes to access services such as schools, doctors and shops, a key aim to ensuring future sustainability.

In 2005, the elected members of Kilkenny Borough Council adopted the City Centre Local Area Plan. The plan establishes a vision for the city centre, to

KILKENNY

In this marble city the fossils sing in the walls.
In the still centre of the comedy festival, a cat smiles.
Why am I happy ? Because I missed the last train home!
Wind quintet for four bus queuers and a breeze.
Ancient and modern: baseball cap caught in the river's light.
Hurling is a kind of opera: discuss. Loudly.
Even the rain wants to make you welcome, tapping your hat.
Sunday morning is the echoing footprint of Saturday night.
We float on beer here, not lost but steering.
Capital of everywhere. Why go anywhere else ?

Kilkenny figure ground plan

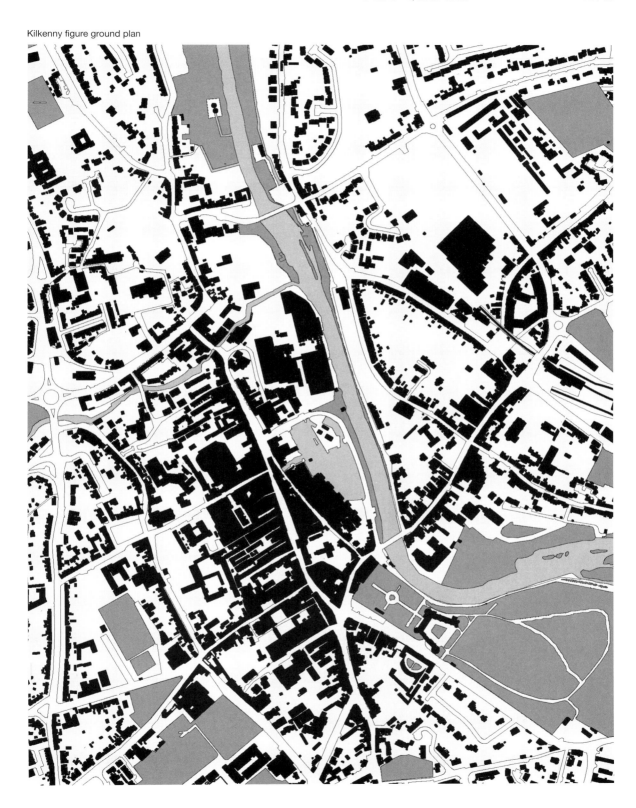

Kilkenny high street

ensure its continued vitality and viability, striking a balance between preserving its architectural and archaeological heritage while facilitating modern living. It concentrates on establishing new linkages, improving permeability, determining suitable uses within the city centre and assesses the existing and future need for car parking.

The basic tourist attraction of Kilkenny is the sheer number and quality of architecturally and historically significant buildings, such as Kilkenny Castle, St. Canice's Cathedral, Rothe House and Shee Alms House; the fine quality of smaller scale elements – shopfronts, houses, slipways, stone walls and general architectural details; the natural beauty of the Nore River Valley; the services provided in the city, including: hotels, guesthouses, restaurants, shops, Design Centre, theatre, galleries, cultural events and the reputation of Kilkenny for arts, culture and crafts; the special attractions such as the Arts Festival, the Cat Laughs Comedy Festival and the Rhythm and Roots Festival; and the bustling nature of the town centre.

One of Kilkenny's strengths is its compact nature, both in physical size and in scale. The pattern of narrow streets with ancient slipways provides an ambience which pedestrians can enjoy, facilitating easy access and movement around the city. The street network has remained largely intact over the centuries. The High Street is a vibrant area, with a mix of uses to attract shoppers and workers.

The historic core – the spine from Kilkenny Castle through High Street, Parliament Street and Irishtown to St. Canice's Cathedral - links these various themes of civic authority and worship. The Tholsel is the seat of local government. With its arcaded front and distinctive bell tower, it has acted as a focal point for local governance for centuries. A long tradition of local politics is maintained to the present day, whilst the civic archive is preserved there as a reminder of the urban history of Kilkenny.

Winchester figure ground plan

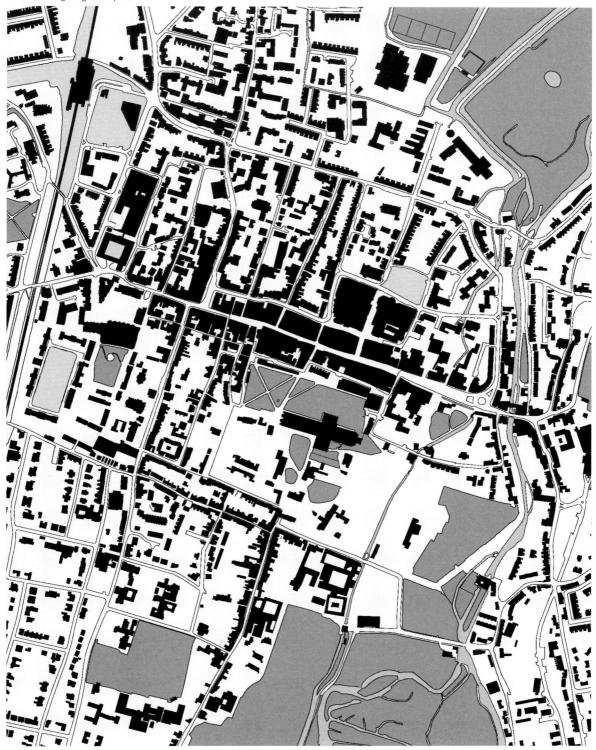

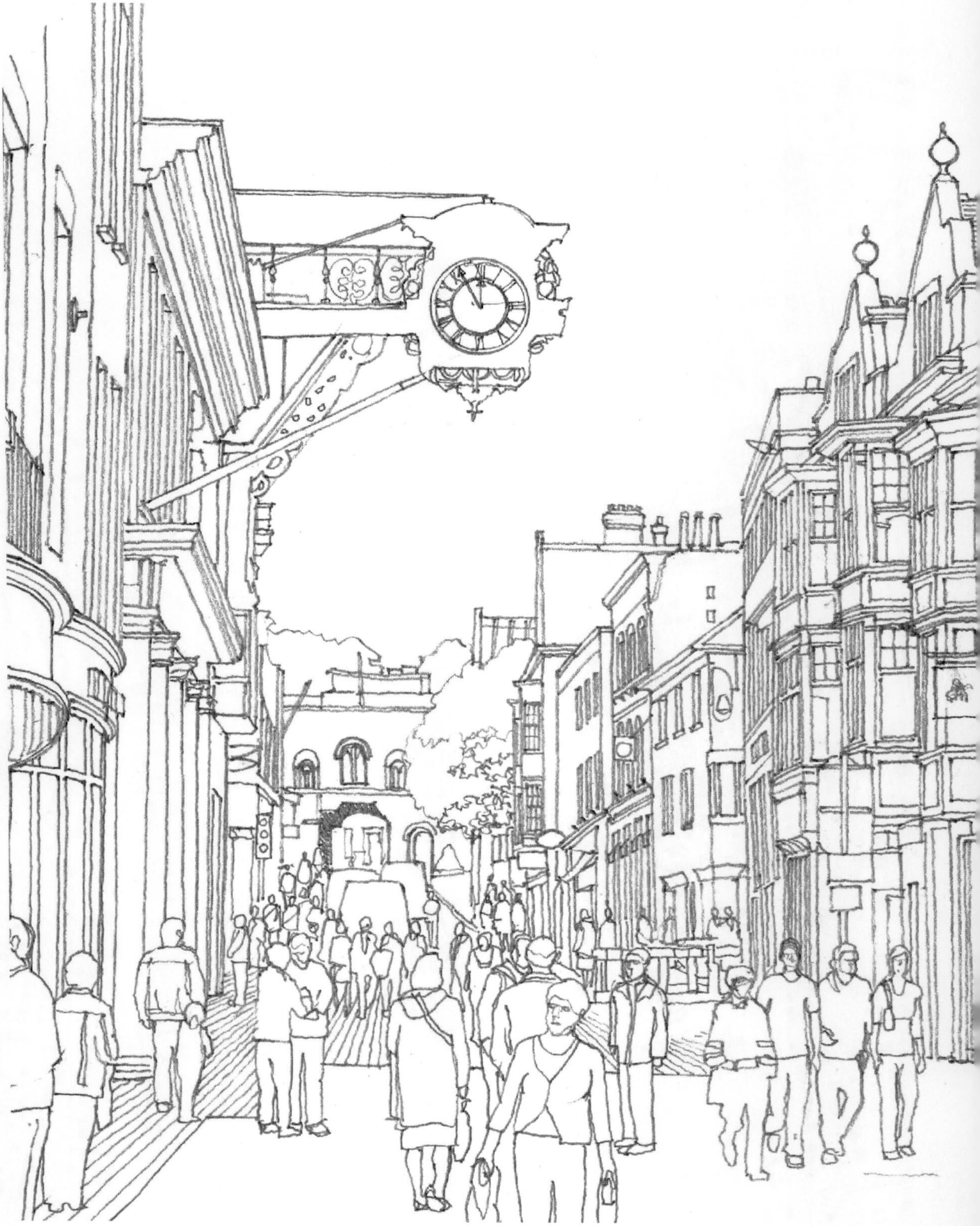

WINCHESTER

Sunday: I heard the bells of the cathedral and they sang. In my heart, in my brain.

Monday: St. Swithin winked and let me off forty days of rain.

Tuesday: Sat in the Royal. Laughed. Cried.

Wednesday: Visited the Gardeners' Question Time Potting Shed. Peeped Inside.

Thursday: Tried to understand the essence of this place of continual renewal and regeneration.

Friday: Decided to stay. Missed the last train at the station.

Saturday: Began to understand that Winchester has no beginning or end.

Sunday: Tear up the diary. Time to spend.

Winchester

The urban form of Winchester has been heavily determined by local topography and geology, with the River Itchen flowing north-south between two opposing hills. The city was founded in the site of a ford across the river, and its urban form is shaped by the historic street pattern that has evolved in response to this context.

Given the compact nature of the city, and the historic streetscape, there is a challenge to manage successfully the daily influx of commuters and visitors. A range of transport management measures have been introduced – park and ride, with buses to key destinations (railway station, shopping centre etc), shopper and visitor car parks, and a cycle-network. This range of initiatives is underpinned by the provision of information including i-kiosks enabling the call-up of local information.

The city is based upon an historic grid layout, with uses subtly but clearly defined – shopping, civic, religious and leisure. The closely laid-out streets, civic spaces and pedestrianised areas all support social interactions.

Winchester is a town whose history and shape have been formed by the great institutions of church, law and military. The largely domestic architecture is set in counterpoint to an impressive cathedral in a modest setting that gives the city a distinctive sense of place, identify and acts for a focus for local life. The whole town acts as a performance space with festivals, street theatre and ice rink inspired Christmas celebrations while the streets, public buildings and green spaces have numerous public art installations produced by the community.

Winchester exhibits a strong sense of place, expressed at the human scale with a very clear expression of civic pride. The university is becoming increasingly important and the town caters for a significant number of visitors each year. Census records reveal that families tend to live in the city for generations; it is also a friendly place with a strong sense of community.

New development in Winchester is influenced by the medieval landscape, with narrow streets opening out into the large spaces around the cathedral and the university. New buildings are carefully integrated into the local environment whilst seeking to meet modern requirements. Services and creative industries in particular are prevalent and unemployment is very low.

Views of Winchester

Views of St. Andrews

St. Andrews

St. Andrews also boasts a distinctive and memorable sense of place with great cultural resonance. It is the 'golf capital of the world', the location of an ancient university, and an outstanding historic town. The centre of St. Andrews has one of the most intensive concentrations of category 'A' and category 'B' listed buildings in Scotland, including landmarks such as the Cathedral, the Castle and the university quadrangles. The town centre is designated as an Outstanding Conservation Area, while the Victorian expansion to the west has conservation area status in its own right.

The economy, society and culture of the town is expressed in its distinctive and beautiful urban form – the pattern of medieval landholdings (riggs) that still determines the urban grain supplemented with cottages of the fishing community and the grander Georgian merchant streets. Culture is expressed today in the activities of the university, the presence of a successful theatre (the Byre), the staging of street events like the annual Lammas Fair (continuously since mediaeval times) and the many golfing tournaments that attract worldwide interest.

There is an active community in St. Andrews and groups such as the St. Andrews Preservation Trust, the East Enders Residents Group, and the Merchants Association, have come together under the banner of 'St. Andrews World Class' to work to promote the interests of the town. There is a strong sense of civic pride, expressed by groups such as St. Andrews in Bloom - which produces a 'blousey' floral programme - and the St. Andrews Preservation Trust, which is ever attentive to new and conservation proposals alike.

Because of the strength of the existing urban form, opportunities for new spaces and buildings are limited but they are generally of high quality, taking reference from local context including detailing and materials. There are good examples of appropriately located contemporary architecture such as the Byre Theatre, a glass restaurant pavilion on the seafront, and the new Arts Faculty building.

St. Andrews' sense of place has a strong relationship with the local topography and geology. The principal streets are aligned along the promontory; the town is flanked by beaches to east and west, and by cliffs to the north. The coastal setting, as a backdrop to the historic skyline, is one of the town's key assets and was immortalised on film in 'Chariots of Fire'.

St. Andrews has adapted to meet changing needs over the centuries, from those of the medieval pilgrims, to the modern day tourists and golfers, with the continuing presence of its ancient university. The stone from the early religious buildings and town walls was recycled into the domestic architecture of Georgian and Victorian houses. Today, imaginative uses are being found for redundant buildings and spaces and the university is taking a lead in pursuing a sustainable agenda in its development programme.

St. Andrews is known as an attractive, safe and enticing place for visitors and residents alike. The town attracts nearly one million visitors each year because of its outstanding historic character, its fine beaches and its reputation as the home of golf. Because of this, visitors come from all over the world as well as locally for day trips. The university plays a key role in the life of the town, with one in every three people on the street a student. It is also sought after as a place to live, with a large residential community still living in the town centre.

The town appeals to people of all ages because of the range of attractions it offers. However, high

property prices make it difficult for low-income families, although many visit its superb beaches, and may stay in the peripheral caravan parks. The demographic of the town is therefore somewhat polarised between students attending the university and the retired or elderly. Fife Council's affordable housing policy is trying to address this issue in new development.

In the town centre, the streets are vibrant due to the combination of uses (retail, commercial and residential) and the pedestrian-friendly environment, with active street frontages arising from traditional building forms and doors and windows onto the street. The high number of residents in the town centre also encourages self-surveillance while active participation by the university in the life of the town assists in promoting civilised and responsible behaviour from students.

East Sands St. Andrews bay and South Street (above)

The Lade Braes is a linear park, running from the edge of town to the centre and well used for informal and formal recreation. The Botanic Gardens and large gardens and semi-public spaces around the Castle and Cathedral are a haven for wildlife and the location for significant trees. The Old Course golf course and the West and East Sands provide tremendous recreation opportunities on either side of the town centre.

Kilkenny has long been a place where cultural pursuits have found expression, from a vibrant crafts environment to theatre and performance art. The Kilkenny Arts Festival continues to thrive with the support of local and state authorities. Kilkenny Borough Council recognises the role being provided by the festival and supports this and other initiatives that provide a platform for the creative arts. Kilkenny Borough Council plays a vital role in maintaining the Watergate Theatre, which provides a venue for the performing arts – drama, dance, and music.

Recreation, whether passive or active, is becoming increasingly important as people become more conscious of leading a healthy lifestyle and Kilkenny is fortunate in having a diverse range of active sporting activities – hurling, rugby, golf, swimming and soccer are all played locally. The development of Kilkenny Castle Park, under the aegis of the Office of Public Works, provides a great urban space close to the town centre.

Winchester, with its strong economic base and large number of visitors, is an attractive place for people to work and visit. The substantial network of medieval streets and buildings and low crime rates make it a safe place to enjoy. Through the university, Winchester attracts young people whilst some 16,000 workers commute daily to the jobs offered in the city, primarily in public administration, the service sector, defence administration, education and tourism. Initiatives such as the Winnall Rock School helps youngsters to acquire music and life skills whilst the theatre has engaged in outreach projects to young children.

Kilkenny (top), Winchester (below)

A strong characteristic of central Winchester is the network of streets fronted by shops, pubs and restaurants. The town centre was (allegedly) the first in the country to be pedestrianised and supports active uses round-the-clock. The active street frontages and the high number of homes within and close to the town centre support self-surveillance. This is reinforced by schemes such as Pubwatch and Shopwatch implemented through the city centre partnership to help local businesses tackle petty crime. The city also has an extensive CCTV network. It also has a fine network of open spaces, in particular around the Cathedral Close that provides opportunity for relaxation within the city itself.

ST. ANDREWS

It's a mixture of sea air, a skyscape
That makes you catch your breath
And those corners, those corners of buildings
That seem to hold history ready
For you to brush against.

It's a montage of the sound
That thinking makes, and a ballscape
That puts three lost round moons
In the bottom of a hedge. Perfect,
I call it. Sea Air, Skyscape, Ballscape, History Corners.

St. Andrews figure ground plan

Winchester is home to a growing number of service and creative industries. There is clear evidence of significant investment in the urban environment, ranging from paving to planting and public art. Commercial activity and prosperity are positively promoted. Current initiatives aimed at supporting the town's economic wellbeing include the Winchester Business Improvement District and the opening of a new Business Centre to support local enterprise.

Business is recognised and promoted through Business Excellence Awards. There are pro-active programmes encouraging economic opportunity, including awards for food businesses. 'Winchester – Towards our Future' is a visioning programme aiming to introduce knowledge and creative industries, supported by the universities.

St. Andrews is also an economic success story, with full employment, a growing research and development sector and strong inward investment. Wealth and employment created in the town percolate throughout a wide hinterland. However, there is as yet no mechanism to enable businesses to contribute to the maintenance and improvement of the urban fabric – business rates are paid at a regional level and cannot be ring-fenced for local use. Nonetheless, many new businesses invest in the town and there is a shortage of suitable premises. The business start-up rate is also well above average while the St. Andrews World Class Initiative brings together employers, public agencies and training providers to deliver training for employees and recruitment support for employers.

Until recently, under-investment in the public realm threatened to jeopardise the success of major investments being made in St. Andrews. Private investment happened in spite of, not because of, public policy. However, there have been more optimistic signs in recent years, including new policies that will emerge through the St. Andrews and East Fife Local Plan and the St. Andrews Design Guidelines that encourage good contemporary design solutions where appropriate.

St. Andrews Golf Course

In 2007 Kilkenny continued to be a place of prosperous commercial activity with investment at an all time high. New commercial developments underway or in the planning stages were seen as ensuring that Kilkenny would be well-placed to avail itself of the economic opportunities of the modern Ireland, at least before the credit crunch. It had been designated as a 'Hub' in the Irish Government's National Spatial Strategy, something that will bring opportunities to underpin its development in the future.

Kilkenny has enjoyed considerable economic growth in the years up to 2007. The city developed and retained firms in growth sectors such as financial services and healthcare. This helped to attract employment and population growth into the city and county.

The town has a strong arts and crafts base that owes its origins to the establishment of Kilkenny Design Workshops in the 1960s - a state-funded body responsible for promoting product and graphic design in industry which operated to the 1980s. The brand also draws on the very strong clusters of creative businesses in and around the city and county - everything from artists to craftspeople, musicians and graphic designers. The Crafts Council of Ireland has been located there since 1998, which has consolidated Kilkenny's position as 'the creative heart of Ireland'.

Technology, tourism, craft & design, engineering and food processing are the dominant industries in the county. Glanbia plc (Kilkenny is the location for the headquarters of the Glanbia multinational food group) and St. Francis Abbey Brewery are major food and beverage companies located in Kilkenny which evolved from the agricultural hinterland. Recently, the River Nore that runs through the centre of Kilkenny was the subject of major works to alleviate flood risk in the City and the opportunity was also taken to develop a linear park along the river providing access and recreation. Environmental sustainability in Kilkenny is pursued through a range

of initiatives including a climate change action plan, a biodiversity action plan, an air quality management plan and the council's sustainability strategy.

Winchester seeks to 'recycle' its buildings by giving them new purposes and uses, particularly through planning and conservation policies, that aim to manage the city's historic environment. Composting and grey water initiatives have also been introduced.

For a town of just 16,000 people, St. Andrews is a remarkably complex urban centre, but its different user groups manage to co-exist harmoniously, with few of the tensions that might be expected in many small towns. Environmental sustainability has not been a priority, but now, led by the progressive university, impressive advances are being made.

The university – which accounts for an estimated 35% of the town's GDP – is acknowledged as the leading British university in terms of sustainable practices of all types, including energy saving, best practice in new build, reducing travel and ethical investments. Fife Council is a leader in recycling and St. Andrews is a designated as a 'Fair Trade' town. However, less positively, visitors and locals have a high degree of car dependence and there has been low participation in green business schemes.

St. Andrews succeeds in maintaining a balance between the needs of its different users – students (who comprise almost 30% of the population in term time), the million visitors annually and the permanent residents – who, thanks to the students and visitors, benefit from a much wider range of amenities, shops, restaurants than they would otherwise enjoy. The social and cultural life of the town, which would otherwise be rather placid, is kept vibrant by students in winter and tourists in summer.

St. Andrews

Kilkenny

Congestion has been an issue for St. Andrews in recent years, but the Transportation Service has been active in making improvements to bus services, connections to the rail network and promoting traffic management including parking, pavement surfacing and cycle provision. There is a good balance of cultural, commercial, retail, and leisure provision to serve residents, visitors, the business community and students.

The approach roads form a radial pattern around the town centre that is laid out to a rough grid pattern, making navigation and orientation easy. Wide pavements and small squares support street activity and social interaction - for example, pavement cafés and events like the Lammas Fair.

Civic, cultural, commercial, retail and leisure facilities are easily accessible in the town centre. There are also a high number of residential properties in the town centre, and the university retains a strong presence here, which adds to its vibrancy. Residential neighbourhoods form an arc of 20th century development south of the town centre.

Transport choices range from the 'Hoppa' bus services from the Park and Ride to key destinations, to dial-a-ride community buses which collect those who need help from home. Fife Council runs a 'bike about' scheme offering free bicycle loans from three destinations in the city.

In Kilkenny, considerable investment and effort are being directed to regeneration and renaissance including McDonagh Junction, a five-hectare site located adjacent to the railway station. The site was once used as the machinery yard for Kilkenny County Council and contained four protected structures in a state of disrepair. Objectives for the site included the preservation of the protected structures, improved accessibility, both vehicular and pedestrian, and the development of a relationship between developers/ investors and the existing community with attendant

potential for socio-economic development. The recent redevelopment of the site includes apartments, a shopping centre, high-tech offices, a hotel, restaurants, recreational, childcare and community facilities. There are two substantial public spaces within the development; one located adjacent to the Goods Shed, a protected structure, and one at the Workhouse Square, also a protected structure.

All three of these towns are economic success stories in their own right. They demonstrate that looking after the sense of place, recognising the qualities of geography and climate as well as (in the cases of St. Andrews and Winchester) maximising the benefits of a university all help to create a distinctive quality of place and of culture. These three towns are microcosms of urbanity, a pleasure to visit and a joy to live in. They demonstrate the best of urbanism in Britain and Ireland at the small scale – and all very worthy of study.

John Worthington

Identity and Branding: What's in a name?

We use words loosely, often forgetting the origins and meaning behind the definition, yet for each of us a word or name can signify a stream of different expectations, associations and remembrances.

In today's increasingly urbanised world, the city has come to signify the clustering of communities for interaction and exchange. With vastly improved physical and virtual connectivity, the sharp definition between urban and rural is blurring. Country living is taking on urban values, whilst city dwellers (often now with one foot in the countryside) are absorbing the interests of rural life. What then, is city identity? How might we define 'place'?

And what defines urbanism and urban settlements? The Academy's Learning from Place initiative aims to celebrate great places at the level of the city, town, neighbourhood, street and place - and learn through example. The Academy's Manifesto for successful urbanism[1] draws on our experience of past successes and reinforces the need for collective vision, human scale, vibrancy of street life, diversity of use, social inclusion, local character and a distinctive identity which sustains a 'sense of collective ownership, belonging and civic pride'. This chapter revisits what we mean by identity, city branding and the sense of place, and sets up some propositions that might help us to evaluate place from the building to the city and to learn from past experience.

Identity can be the characteristics of a place that makes it memorable, or even forgettable, as well as the names or symbols that turn identity into a brand. The brand in turn signifies what the city wishes others to recognise it stands for. The name of Venice is universally recognized as being associated with the past, merged with culture, relaxation and pleasure. Each of us, influenced by the PR

Amsterdam

Amsterdam

proposition for the place, will have our own bundle of attributes gleaned from newspaper articles, images, conversations, a special visit, or perhaps a life of being there. In reality, like maps, there is no definitive description of a place; it depends on whose eyes, expectations and values it is being seen through. The Japanese, when describing a concept, encapsulate it in an evocative word or symbol that can cover a wide spectrum of interpretation to which each individual can then attach their own meaning and memories. A 'key word' is likened to a carrier bag with the name and logo on the side, within which can be put the attributes appropriate to the individual's perception at that moment in time.

As urbanists, we are keen to suggest that we are also place-makers. This is a brave assertion. It could be argued that architects design meaningful spaces that support the activity of people and institutions to make memorable places. J.B. Jackson, one of North America's most insightful commentators on the urbanising landscape of the mid-twentieth century, reflected on the overuse of a 'sense of place'[2] as an expression used "chiefly by architects but taken over by urban planners and interior decorators and the promoters of condominiums,

so it now means very little." To understand the concept better, Jackson went back to the classical concept of genius loci derived from the unique quality of being the guardian of the spirit of that place. The age of the Enlightenment rejected the 'divine or supernatural' and referred to 'the genius of a place' for its meaning and influence. Perhaps today it would reflect its atmosphere and quality of environment. Jackson suggests that one way of describing such a locality would be to say "they are cherished because they are embedded in the everyday world around us and easily accessible, but at the same time are distinct from that world. A visit to one of them is a small but significant event". Perhaps most poignantly, Jackson reminds us that "the average American still associates a sense of place not so much with architecture or a monument or a designed space as with some event, some daily or weekly or seasonal occurrence which we look forward to or remember and which we share with others, and as a result the event becomes more significant than the place itself." Well-considered, meaningful spaces enhance and support the experience, but only when they are brought alive by time and the introduction of memory.

It is clear that cities, and place-making within them, are a complex combination of physical interjections, organisational processes, and individual commitment layered through time. The search for a conceptual framework for what makes 'good city form' has a long tradition through the writings of those such as Camillo Sitte, Raymond Unwin, De Cronin Hastings in his special editions of the Architectural Review on Townscape[3], Ed Bacon in Philadelphia[4] and the work of Kevin Lynch[5]. In Britain, Lynch's theory of what makes good city form has become mainstream thinking through the government planning guidance 'By Design'[6]. It is reinforced by The Academy of Urbanism Manifesto. These are excellent foundations, but how do we ensure that we continue to test the theories, recognise where new conditions are emerging and avoid becoming slaves to perceived wisdom? The Academy is committed to asking questions and "seek[s] to create a body of evidence-based enquiry that can inform our quest to identify and deliver best practice in Urbanism[7]." Initiatives such as UniverCities linked with the annual awards are moving to support this quest, and offer exciting opportunities to enlarge the debate.

The format of The Urbanism Awards covers a wide scale from the single identifiable space with its five categories: Place, e.g. Somerset House Courtyard, or the Great Hall of the British Museum, to Cities, where the named city is now inextricably linked with a wider networked metropolitan region. New city regions are emerging such as the Øresund (Copenhagen, Malmö), The Ruhrgebiet (Essen, Duisburg, and Dusseldorf) or the Bay Area (San Francisco, Oakland and San José) which as Jane Jacobs explains in Cities and the Wealth of Nations[8] are working within their own economies as 'city states' within a global economy.

How we assess the quality of our cities will increasingly be informed by how we perceive their role, functions and meaning. As accessibility between places increases with the take-up of information and communications technology, so our perceptions of the city change. Traditional administrative boundaries become blurred, as cities shatter into networked conurbations. How we use and define the city is both virtual and physical. The citizen perceives his or her city from at least three different perspectives:

- The city of their imagination where, with instant Internet access anywhere in the world, personal contact can be on their doorstep[9];

- The city of convenience; spread over a metropolitan region accessible by good public transport where we can find what we need, most economically convenient;

- The city of place - locations within cities with distinctive character and recognisable qualities.

Each of us, depending on our values, interests and expectations, has a different perception of what constitutes the city. These perceptions can be given form through 'mind maps' that have no scale and may have little relevance to political boundaries, but do reflect how individuals use, experience and understand the city.

To help to understand the different perceptions of Osaka, the municipality undertook a pilot study[10] where a cross-section of outsiders were asked to draw a map of their Osaka. These maps highlighted the importance of railways, highways, parks and boulevards as the structure of the city, with many centres for different functions that overlapped across administrative boundaries. The visiting architect's remembrance was of iconic buildings, fun and a green structuring boulevard. The resident business executive perceived a financial focus defined by dollar signs and connectivity to the Kansai region and the world. The graduate architect working in the city whilst 'sleeping' in the region, perceived a diverse 'funky' urban centre at the heart of a global conurbation.

Clearly, city identity is a combination of the aspirations and experiences of the citizens and those who visit. The sense of place and identity is reflected in an understanding of both the wider city region and specific physical places. For each city to find its authentic and distinctive identity in a 'placeless world', where the same brands occur on every high street, is the challenge. It is too easy to revert to historical urban centres as the only reflection of successful towns and cities.

The five categories of awards the Academy presents are not distinct but interrelated, all contributing to the identity and sense of place of a particular town or city, which is composed of places, streets and neighbourhoods.

Places as spaces, can be both public (Trafalgar Square, or North Laine,

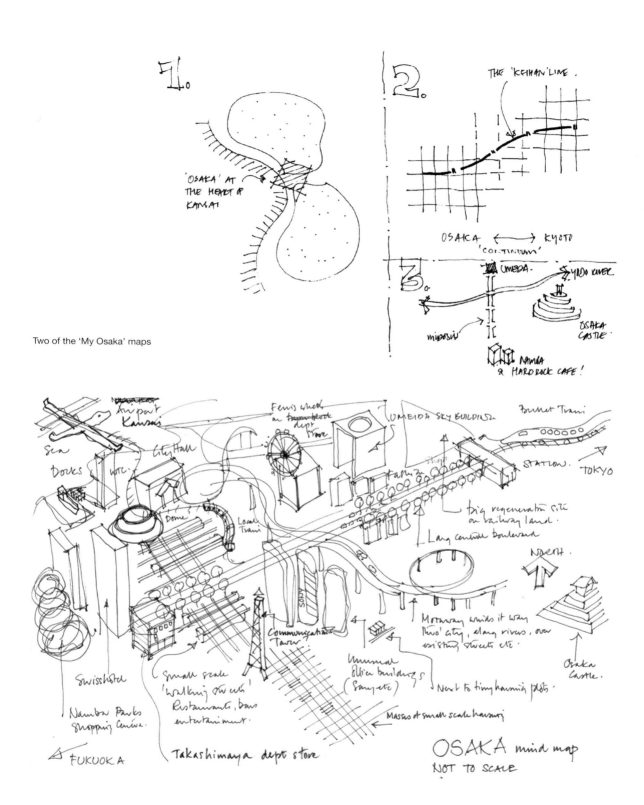

Two of the 'My Osaka' maps

Brighton) or semipublic (Great Court, British Museum or Oxford Castle) within a building or defined by buildings. Maarten Hajer and Arnold Reijndorp in their analysis of what makes good public space[11] identify three key factors that define the public realm:

- Loose fit, with an ambiguity of functions, not precisely designed to fit each use;
- Distinctive areas, each with a dominant culture, with a focus on the overlap between the different cultures;
- Space which is governed and managed by the community, and accessible to all, 24 hours a day, seven days a week - '24/7', as the Americans would have it.

By contrast, the semi-public realm tends to be precisely designed to meet exacting functional requirements; homogeneous in its rentals, demographics and mix of functions – and themed.

Successful public places are full of paradoxes, "Citizens create meaningful public space by expressing their attitudes, asserting their claims and using it for their own purposes."[12] The distinctive use of that space becomes more pleasant "the more the activities of the dominant group turn out to be variants on one's own everyday life, and thus foster participation rather than spectatorship".

Streets are the glue that holds the city together, along which distinctive places may occur. Streets may be either thoroughfares – the route to or between places (Great West Road and The Mall in London) – or linear activities such as the seaside promenade (Bridlington), the high street (Deal), the market (Portobello Road, London) or a formal setting (Royal Crescent, Bath)

Neighbourhoods are the distinctive quarters of a community which draw their identity from the dominant function - living, employment, education or leisure; mix of activities, demographics, and physical setting. Successful cities are dependent on the quality and diversity of their neighbourhoods and the streets and places within them.

The identity of the community, city or town and its perceived success depends on the values it sets out to respond to, the quality of its social, political and physical infrastructure, and its approach to governance.

If the evaluation of what makes a good or bad place is dependent on the values of the particular community and the individuals within it, then one could argue that there is no one answer but only appropriate solutions for a moment in time.

Evaluation, Measurement and Feedback

To give some structure to the evaluation of best practice and to help understand what makes good places, there are three levels of analysis needed:

1. The underlying principles, that are recognised as being the key factors in achieving successful urban form and a sense of place, regardless of context and culture. Kevin Lynch sets five basic performance dimensions: Vitality, Sense, Fit, Access, Control, and two metacriteria - Efficiency and Justice: the way in which environmental benefits and costs are distributed. Lynch proposes Justice "is the criterion which balances the gains among persons while efficiency balances the gains among the different values."[13]

2. The specific attributes for a particular context, which may vary depending on the values and expectations of the user. If the aspirations of the individual or community for minimum change and organic growth, then being well-connected, with diverse cultures and outside investment might not be the appropriate attributes to pursue.

3. The integrating systems for governance, capacity building and changing perceptions. What then might be the most appropriate measures for analysis, improvement and comparison? And how can these be expressed so they become part of a feedback and learning loop to ensure continuous improvement?

The design professions are familiar with the measurement of areas and the use of graphics to present and make comparisons between projects. Figure ground plans are a common means of comparing the grain, massing and permeability of neighbourhoods. Plot ratios, site coverage, pie charts of the allocation of functions (roads, green space, building footprint) are well-established measures for comparison and evaluation. However, what is less clear is whether these are the most important characteristics to measure, and how valuable they are without understanding the context and output they achieve. Seldom do we see the use of socio-economic measures, the performance of the neighbourhood or its users, linked to spatial yardsticks to understand better the relationship between urban form and organisational performance. Figure ground drawings give us a bird's eye perspective of the neighbourhood. What they do not provide is an understanding of the interaction of the public and semi-public from the perspective of the pedestrian. The divisions between public, semi-public, privileged and private space are blurring. Large building blocks are becoming more permeable as corporations and institutions recognise the value of collaboration, interaction and openness. In the future, groundscape plans which show both external and internal public and semi-public routes may be of increasing relevance in our understanding of how the city functions. DEGW's proposals for the British Library, like Nolli's plan for Rome, represents a different

An analysis of the a 500m square drawn around DEGW's London (top) and New York (bottom) offices.

- Pedestrianised spaces
- Footpaths
- Roads
- Public space within buildings
- Private space within buildings
- Green space
- Doors

perspective of the St. Pancras/King's Cross area when the semi-public areas within the station and library are drawn.

Through the Internet, potential sources for data are myriad. Combined with on-site observation, the availability of data is not a problem. The challenge will be to recognise which data are most relevant to collect in order to infer improvements to future design and performance, to say nothing of how to communicate the findings most effectively. Knowing the measurable physical attributes of a site, such as site coverage, plot ratio, and block size, are most valuable when combined with other measures of social or economic performance, such as rental return.

Place measures that combine spatial and organisational characteristics of an area are of value in:

- Monitoring performance for existing neighbourhoods or design proposals
- Bench marking against other locations to assess performance
- Setting standards against which to perform

Evidence-based decision making for planning and design is gathering momentum, but is still largely reliant on anecdotal examples of what we like, with little supporting evidence. What we perceive is often very different to what we actually do in practice. DEGW has shown there can be a 40% difference between how users perceive they use their space and what is actually happening in practice. Better data are critical if we are to make improvements and question perceived wisdom.

Identity and Brand

The identity of a place is the meaning each individual gives to that place or object. It is a combination of the physical heritage, local culture, and geographical context, overlaid with perceived remembrances. It is argued by some that identity is in fact merely personal remembrances. Identity has been described as both a sense of purpose and a strong sense of belonging[14]. A city brand might be described as the reinterpretation of its identity to reflect the city's aspirations and values in a way that it would like to be perceived by visitors, outside investors, and its inhabitants.

Successful brands as a reflection of a city's identity are more than simply a slogan or logo. The 'Big Apple' universally reminds us of the vibrancy, confidence and wholeness of Manhattan, which is reflected in community behaviour, the quality of its buildings and the character of its street life. Tradition and the connection with the past are celebrated in festivals, which all reinforce the brand.

Brands can be both a source of differentiation and identification. As cities become increasingly homogenised through a process of globalisation, what makes them special is the continuity of local tradition, the character of the architecture, the values reflected through local governance and the diversity of the community stimulated by the breaking down of transnational boundaries. Melbourne, a city where over three hundred languages are spoken, celebrates its diversity through its variety of foods and café culture. Copenhagen has created an identity around its concern for the human scale. Amsterdam is recognised for its open society and entrepreneurial spirit. Edinburgh stands for tradition and the arts through its annual festival. The brand cannot merely change and reinforce external perceptions, but it also strengthens the confidence and sense of belonging of those who live there. Glasgow's witty campaign for 'Glasgow's Miles Better' transmitted a strong sense of confidence and was supported by a robust programme of milestone events, beginning with the Garden Festival (1988) through the European City of Culture (1990) to the Year of Architecture (1999).

Architectural icons, often linked with the regeneration of a redundant industrial area, are too often seen as the instant panacea. The harbourside in Baltimore or the Guggenheim in Bilbao succeeded through strong leadership, community commitment and thoughtful design. Iconic architecture will not work if simply planted. Sydney's Opera House and its bridge now personify the city, whereas Calatrava's spiral tower at Malmö is alien to its context, and projects mixed messages.

What then makes a brand authentic? Personality is not formed instantaneously - it needs nurturing and assimilation, to raise awareness externally and at the same time give ownership and meaning to the local community. City Branding, a programme initiated by the Netherlands Foundation for Visual Arts, Design and Architecture[15], brought together a group of young architects to visualise eight cities in the Netherlands. The results recognised that with rapid growth the essence of these cities often resided at their perimeter and not at the historical centre, and the vitality was emanating from the recent arrivals. Heerlen, a city of just less than 100,000 situated on the southern edge of the country, has a reputation for high unemployment and drug abuse. Within its wider context, it is part of a rich and diverse urban/rural continuum. The proposed re-envisioning focuses on the theme 'Parkstad Limburg', an exclamation mark that contains a strong park atmosphere as well as a convincing urban centre. Almere is a city that has grown from nothing to a population of over 150,000 in thirty years. The character of the city is being formed by its pioneering spirit and constant change. Breda, a historic city now with over 150,000 inhabitants and high-speed rail links is 'ambitiously aiming for a new position in the region and the European context'. It is searching for a new definition to focus change. Its new slogan 'Breda - City with an Open Character' aims to align the city's historical and geographical attributes with its political attitude and actual atmosphere to 'shape a new character appreciating openness and exchange'.

In conclusion - understanding better what we have, how it works and where we can improve are all at the heart of identity, and these can be expressed through a brand. In the spirit of opening the debate and enquiry, three questions are posed for future research:

- What are the key, universally applicable characteristics of a 'good place' - the most meaningful descriptors?

- What methods of representation would be best to enable comparative analysis?

- How well do these match our current perception of what makes a successful place?[16]

One word or image can synthesize a complex set of impressions. New York's 'I♥NY' campaign focused on the symbol of the Big Apple, encapsulated visitors' expectations and gave renewed confidence to a centre which had been losing its residential population. On the other hand, Bilbao has become synonymous with Frank Gehry's Guggenheim Museum – the architectural cuckoo, where the trophy dwarfs the place. Both these examples represent catalysts of change and metaphors for the cities' ambitions, but they tell only part of the story. How we perceive towns and cities is a complex web of experiences and impressions. Our perceptions of exemplary cities and towns is about the integrating systems they provide and the brand image they project.

References
1. John Thompson Space, Place, Life; Introduction & Manifesto, The Academy for Urbanism, London 2006
2. J.B.Jackson A Sense of PLACE a Sense of TIME. Yale University Press, 1994
3. Nicolas Baumann Townscape in Urban Conservation, Doctoral Dissertation, Institute of Advanced Architectural Studies, University of York, 1996 (Excellent review of the major theorists on urban form and Townscape from the late 19th Century)
4. Edmund Bacon Design of Cities, Thames and Hudson, London 1967
5. Much of the best of Kevin Lynch's insightful work is in his collected writing. Kevin Lynch Good City Form MIT Press, Cambridge 1984, and Banerjee & Southwood (editors) City Sense and City Design, MIT Press 1990
6. By Design
7. John Thompson Space, Place, Time, The Academy for Urbanism, London 2006
8. Jane Jacobs Cities and the Wealth of Nations, Social Science 1985
9. Web sites such as Second Life and web-based games like Legends 2 are creating a virtual world, with places of the imagination that are being traded for real money
10. John Worthington My Osaka: A report for Osaka City, DEGW, London 2005
11. Maarten Hajer & Arnold Reijndorp In Search of a New Public Domain, NAi Publishers Rotterdam 2001
12. Ibid
13. Kevin Lynch Good City Form, MIT Press Cambridge 1984 (Part 2: A Theory of Good City Form
14. Wally Olins Corporate Identity, Thames and Hudson London 1994
15. Urban affairs/Veronique Patteeuw City Branding: Image Building and Building Images, NAI Publishers, Rotterdam 2002
16. John Billingham and Richard Cole The Good Place Guide: Urban Design in Britian and Ireland, Batsford, London 2002

David Rudlin

The three ages of a creative quarter

Soho, Temple Bar & Grainger Town

What is a neighbourhood? If a neighbourhood is a place containing 'neighbours' - a district where people get on, where there are social interactions and a sense of community, then the three shortlisted neighbourhoods in the 2008 Academy of Urbanism Awards are not really neighbourhoods. At least that is not the thing that makes Grainger Town in Newcastle, Soho in London and Temple Bar in Dublin great. What they are is great creative quarters, which is something quite different.

Soho is perhaps the nearest of the three to a true neighbourhood, having been a residential community for centuries. However, Temple Bar and, the 2008 winner, Grainger Town, are areas that are emerging as residential quarters as well as also being many other things. Both were run-down and under threat twenty years ago and both are remarkable regeneration success stories. They are neighbourhoods as well as being thriving mixed-use, creative and entertainment districts in the heart of their respective cities. This is more than just semantics; in many respects, a creative quarter is the opposite of a neighbourhood because it is the sort of place where you can do stuff that you wouldn't perhaps want your neighbours to see. Creative urban quarters like Greenwich Village in New York, the Rive Gauche in Paris or Kreutzberg in Berlin are the places where you go to escape the strictures of the neighbourhood of your parents. They are

Three very different creative quarters, Temple Bar (top), Grainger Town (middle) and Soho (bottom)

places where you can find the freedom to express yourself, to meet new people, to be bad! Neighbourhoods are great for growing up and growing old but for that short burst or rebellion in between, you need the anonymity, diversity and sheer excitement of a creative urban quarter. This is what the three districts shortlisted for The Great Neighbourhood Award really are – good places to be bad, or creative, or both.

Even better, the three areas represent three stages in the evolution of a creative quarter. Soho belongs on the list of the world's great bohemian quarters. Carnaby Street is a centre for the city's fashion industry, while Soho also includes important theatres such as the Palladium and the Lyric as well as the more recent Soho Theatre, home to new theatre and stand-up comedy, and music venues from Ronnie Scotts to the clubs where the Rolling Stones, the Kinks and the Sex Pistols played. It is the centre of the capital's gay community, and a series of embattled ethnic communities being squeezed out by rising values as well as a growing affluent population. On top of all this, Soho is still a centre for the sex trade and (for different reasons) a major tourist destination. All of this contained in an uneasy state of balance within a small piece of real estate in central London, making Soho unlike anywhere else in Britain.

Outwardly, Temple Bar in Dublin has many similarities to Soho. It is a heady mixture of culture and hedonism with creative industries existing side by side with hen parties, drunkenness and harassed residents. However, while the quarter may have a long history, Temple Bar today is the creation of the last twenty years. It is indeed an accidental creation, born out of attempts to demolish the area to create a bus station. The temporary uses allowed to occupy property prior to demolition took root to such an extent that a campaign to save the area gained official support and gave birth to the culture-led regeneration of the area. Today the issues are like those faced by the gardener who, having worked for years to establish a series of plants, sees some of them growing so vigorously

that they threaten to squeeze out the other species. Temple Bar has suffered from its 'Party Capital' reputation; streets smelling of vomit and urine are hardly conducive to cultural uses or residents. Temple Bar is still in its raw state before history and tradition have mediated these conflicts as they have done in Soho.

The winner of The Great Neighbourhood Award, Grainger Town in Newcastle is the youngster of the three in terms of its development, and also the most beautiful. Like the other two areas, it has its fair share

The Temple Bar (top), Carnaby Street in Soho (middle) and Thomas Heatherwick's Blue Carpet on the edge of Grainger Town (bottom)

of hedonism in the shape of the Bigg Market, famous for boys in tee-shirts and girls in mini-skirts braving sub-zero temperatures on a winter's evening. It was built as a genteel residential and business district and away from the mayhem of the Bigg Market it largely retains this character. Twenty years ago, it was, like Temple Bar, run down and largely vacant. Its regeneration has been engineered by the public sector and the impetus was to find new uses for its fine stock of buildings. This has included investment in new apartments, offices and leisure uses and the area has been more than saved, it has been turned into one of the most interesting quarters in Newcastle, without the intense pressures of Temple Bar or Soho.

These three creative quarters have become central to the economic revival of their host cities. Back in the early 1990s when the regeneration of Grainger Town and Temple Bar started, economic policy was still focussed on manufacturing. Over the intervening years this has been supplanted by knowledge industries, creative business and the service sector. Initially, it seemed that information technology, by allowing people to work from wherever they wished,

would exacerbate the problems of the older industrial cities. However, something strange started to happen in the 1990s. These same cities stopped being the source of economic problems and started to become the drivers of regional economic growth.

As manufacturing is off-shored, economic success depends on knowledge, innovation and creativity. These qualities are found in cities, particularly those with great creative quarters. Richard Florida, in a series of books on the Creative Class,[1] has shown through analysis of satellite photography that more than two-thirds of the world's output is now generated in just 40 city-region clusters - even with their higher costs. The reason why it is worth paying more to be in these cities is the competitive advantage of 'cognitive diversity'. In simple terms, the greater the range of people you have available to you, the better placed you are to solve problems, come up with new ideas and to exploit them efficiently. Indeed, Florida finds a strong correlation between the size of a city's creative class, the ethnic and sexual diversity of its population, the level of innovation as measured by patents, and the new business formation rate as measured by VAT registrations. Cities therefore need to attract and retain this creative class.

What role do creative quarters play in this process? The members of the creative class may not want to live in a creative quarter (they would never all fit!) but they are likely to be drawn to cities with a strong creative ambience and with a range of cultural and leisure activities that they find attractive. Creative quarters are therefore an important part of a city's offer. They are also the place from which new ideas emerge. It's ironic that the alternative quarters, artists colonies and squats that have in the past been tolerated at best may hold the key to the future economic success of the city. The people attracted to these bohemian places are just the sort of people who will make a difference in the future. What then can we learn from the three creative quarters shortlisted for the Academy awards?

Grainger Town

Grainger Town lies at the heart of Newcastle, stretching up the hill from the station to include the Theatre Royal, the Grainger Market and St. Mary's Cathedral. The quarter covers much of the eastern side of the city centre, including upmarket stores, professional offices, new apartments and a wide range of eating and drinking establishments from the exclusive to the 'lively'.

The area originated in the 1830s when the architect-developer Richard Grainger won what would now be called a masterplanning competition to create an extension to the medieval city. Grainger Town is probably best known for Grey Street, voted the finest street in Britain on a number of occasions and described by Gladstone in 1862 as 'our best modern street'. The street curves upwards to Grey's Monument, a 134-foot column topped by a statue of Earl Grey. The neighbourhood created by Grainger was integrated into the surrounding area, particularly the city's medieval Bigg Market. Though built at the beginning of the Victorian era, Grainger

preferred Georgian architecture and Grainger Town owes much to the Georgian grandeur of Edinburgh New Town or Bath, both built in the previous century. It is an extraordinarily coherent architectural district with 450 buildings, 244 of which are listed.

Like all cities, Newcastle has suffered from insensitive planning and architecture over the years. One of the worst intrusions was the redevelopment of the Georgian buildings around Eldon Square, just to the north of Grainger Town, with a windowless shopping mall. Grainger Town largely escaped this destruction but succumbed instead to economic decline. By the early 1990s, there was one million square feet of vacant space in the area and 47% of its listed buildings were considered to be at risk. The Grainger Town Project was established in 1997 as a partnership between the City Council, English Heritage and English Partnerships. The project ran until 2003 investing some £40 million of public funds. The achievements of the project are impressive: over 1,500 jobs; 286 new businesses; 80,900

The glories of Grainger Town; Central Arcade (above) and Grey Street (opposite)

Grainger Town figure ground plan

GRAINGER TOWN, NEWCASTLE

From a place North of heaven
Richard Grainger looks down
On the rebuilding and remaking of Grainger Town.

From a place North of success
You can see how the future
Has grown from something you could call a mess.

From a place North of heaven
Richard Grainger is smiling
As the streets that he built
Are unwinding and gleaming
And mending and healing
And if history imposes
A dust-laden ceiling
Then Grainger Town's breaking
It down as it's growing...

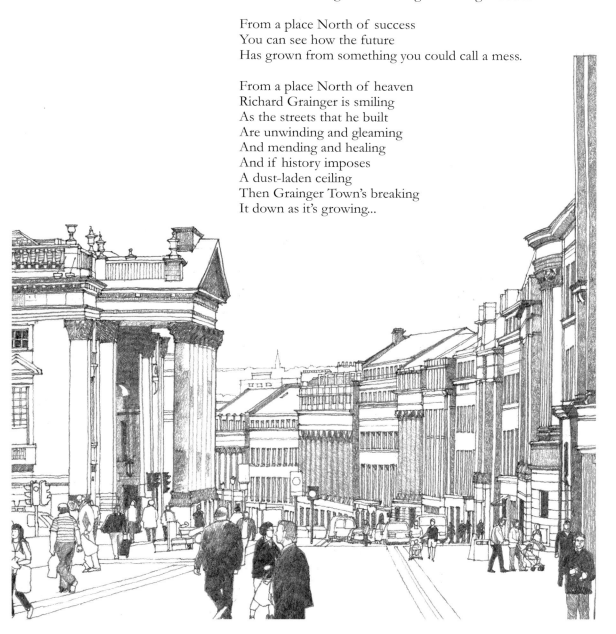

square metres of new and improved commercial floor space and just under 600 apartments. Altogether, 121 buildings have been brought back into active use, including most of the buildings at risk. The results can be seen today in an area that is thriving and prosperous, with lively streets and well-refurbished buildings on beautifully-proportioned streets given back their architectural coherence and unity.

From the outset, the project was focused on the architectural heritage as well as economic regeneration. This was perhaps unsurprising given the project's partners and the wealth of listed buildings in the area. The public realm improvements are understated and stylish and the historic buildings have been lovingly and faithfully restored. There are good examples of contemporary design, particularly the interior of buildings such as the refurbished Assembly Rooms. However, the project can perhaps be criticised for being slightly over-reverent to history and therefore conservative in its outlook. The planners, for example resisted an application for banners to be hung between the columns of the portico of the Theatre Royal on conservation grounds. Comparing this attitude to contemporary architecture in Temple Bar and Grainger Town can have the feeling of a museum piece which is not ideal for a creative quarter.

However, the revival of the area is unmistakable. Retailing that had died back in the north of the area has revived strongly along Grainger Street and new retail space has been created. The area has also re-established its role as a location for professional offices as well as developing strong cultural and evening uses. At its heart sits the Bigg Market, infamous for hard drinking and night clubs. This continues as strongly as it ever did and the remarkable thing is how little it affects the character of the rest of the area and generally there are not the conflicts between different uses found in Temple Bar or Soho. This is perhaps because Grainger Town is large enough to absorb its different uses and the scale of its streets is also an advantage. However, there is much that other quarters could learn from its success in absorbing so much activity in such a harmonious way.

The view from the cramped platform at the top of Grey's Monument (opposite) and other views of Grainger Town (above)

Temple Bar

There is allegedly a cycle of decline and renewal that takes place in cities. Neighbourhoods fall into decline. The availability of cheap space means that they are colonised by artists. Gradually the area becomes fashionable in a counter-culture sort of way. This causes values to rise attracting the attention of developers and more established companies. Over time, this investment gathers pace, more and more people are attracted to the area, squeezing out the artists that started the process. The result is that the excitement that initially attracted people is sanitised and eventually extinguished. This process can be seen at work in cities across the world, Covent Garden is perhaps the most extreme UK example of the phenomenon. A truly great neighbourhood would capture the power of this process without being spoiled by it. In Dublin, Temple Bar comes close to doing this.

Temple Bar, named after Sir William Temple, has been part of historic Dublin for centuries. However, in the late 1970s, much of it was designated for clearance to make way for a bus station, and the state-owned transport company, CIE, started buying up properties. Rather than demolishing buildings as they were acquired, CIE made the 'mistake' of letting them on short leases. Over a relatively short period, something interesting started to emerge.

The area became a base of artists and independent shops and soon these new businesses started a campaign to save it from demolition. This culminated in 1991 when the Irish Government reprieved the area and designated it as Dublin's cultural quarter. The properties acquired by CIE were transferred to Temple Bar Properties, a regeneration agency set up to manage the renewal of the area. As a major landowner, the agency had considerable assets and financial muscle and was responsible for kick-starting a remarkable transformation, with the aid of urban renewal tax incentives.

One of the first things it organised was an international design competition for the area, won by a consortium of local architectural practices calling themselves Group 91. Their masterplan is an excellent combination of careful urbanism and contemporary design. It identified the main weakness of the neighbourhood as a lack of public realm and proposed a series of public spaces, enclosed by new buildings. The main elements were Temple

Temple Bar remains lively whatever the time of day or weather

Temple Bar figure ground plan

TEMPLE BAR, DUBLIN

Consider this: it nearly became a bus station.
This focal point of a vibrant dancing nation
    Almost became a place for queueing
    And studying timetables on shelters.

But look at it now: the music, the singing,
The way the laughter bounces around the sky
Then comes back on itself and chimes
In the glass of an upheld glass that seems to play
A note that you can only hear on Temple Bar.

And it could all have been so different:
The bus reversing, the passengers standing
And waiting. The fumes. The low hum.

Bar Square, a new curving street to increase permeability and Meeting House Square with its outdoor cinema and public stage. Also at the heart of the plan was a programme of public investment in twelve cultural institutions, nine of which have survived. Today, Temple Bar is home to the Irish Photographic Archive, Gallery and School, the Irish Film Institute, FilmBase, the Project Arts Centre, the Gaiety School of Acting, the Ark children's cultural centre and the Contemporary Music Centre. Each of these is housed in a new or refurbished building, many designed by the practices that made up Group 91. The new buildings are without exception contemporary in design, winning 25 national and international architectural awards and showing that good modern architecture can enhance a historic urban area. Temple Bar is home to over 50 cultural and arts organisations and 2,000 residents. The Temple Bar Cultural Trust (successor to Temple Bar Properties) runs almost 400 free cultural events a year attended by more than 600,000 people.

There is, and always has been, another side to Temple Bar – alongside the cultural institutions are found the bars and clubs that have long been part of the area. These bars have participated fully in the area's regeneration, using tax incentives to refurbish, develop and extend their premises. As a result, Dublin - and Temple Bar, in particular - became a 'party capital' attracting 'stag nights' and 'hen parties' flown in on cheap flights – usually from England. To the visitor, the Temple Bar experience includes the pubs, the galleries, buskers on the streets, public art, specialist shops and free events. However, it is difficult to keep these elements in balance and recently the bars have threatened to overwhelm the other uses. Moves have been made to persuade the publicans to discourage the hen and stag trade and in any case cities like Prague and Amsterdam have taken over the 'party city' mantle.

In many respects, these are the problems of success. Many run down urban quarters would love to

suffer from too much vitality! However, they do illustrate that the process of regeneration, once started, is not easy to control. Temple Bar is a small area, covering just 24 acres, and yet has developed three very successful roles: cultural quarter, residential neighbourhood and leisure destination. As a result, it bustles with life and crackles with tension in just the way that cities should. In this respect, it is similar to Soho and it is sobering to think that all this has been achieved in just fifteen years. Whether the three roles are sustainable in the long-term remains to be seen. There is certainly a need for greater collaboration and urban management to resolve the inevitable tensions. However, the tensions will never be removed, indeed if they were the area would lose much of what makes Temple Bar a great neighbourhood.

Temple Bar has seen an extraordinary amount of investment in cultural institutions that sit alongside the traditional bars (bottom left)

Soho

The original creative quarter, Soho illustrates all of the characteristics that such quarters need, as well as the tensions and contradictions that they must face. Covering just over 100 acres in central London, it contains huge variations from the smart media hub of Soho Square, to the revitalised fashion shops of Carnaby Street, China Town, London's main gay village on Old Compton Street and the remnants of the sex industry around Brewer Street and Berwick Street. Soho has been a 'creative quarter' for more than 300 years. Prior to its development in the 1660s, it was a royal hunting ground; 'So Ho' is apparently the cry that the huntsmen made when in pursuit of their quarry. It was originally planned as an affluent middle-class neighbourhood like the nearby districts of Mayfair and Fitzrovia. However, a series of botched property deals meant that Soho had soon degenerated into a low-price district, a place where immigrants and artists could afford to get a toe-hold near to the centre of the city. Early residents included Huguenots fleeing France, Italians, Germans, Greeks and Russians and more recently Chinese, Asian and Somali immigrants, all of whom have left their mark on the area.

Soho hasn't entirely excised the sex industry (opposite), even if some of it is more mainstream today. It is still home to a large working class community housed in schemes like the housing association project (below).

Many of the early groups were artisans and Soho became known for its small workshops. It was this that attracted artists like Constable and Canaletto and, more recently, Francis Bacon and Lucien Freud to set up their studios there. Its pubs have long had the reputation as drinking dens for many less-distinguished artists and writers. Soho has long been known for its cosmopolitan character, its 'liveliness' and its hedonism. This may have attracted artists but it also had a seedier side and from the mid-18th century the neighbourhood became known for the sex trade. This was at its height in the 1970s when there were more than 250 establishments in the area, including sex shops, revue bars, 'clip joints' and adult cinemas. It became

known for crime and exploitation and was the haunt of gangsters and starlets. Since then, the sex industry has been brought under control through licensing and the prosecution of 'clip joints'. It is now found in just a small area around the junction of Brewer Street and Berwick Street. The dilemma faced by Westminster Council in drawing up its Soho Action Plan in 2006 is the extent to which this activity is part of the heritage of the area – would Soho be Soho without the sex?

The decline of Carnaby Street has been reversed by Soho Estates, which bought the freehold ten years ago. Through careful management of the portfolio,

Soho figure ground plan

SOHO, LONDON

I'm rushing down Beak Street to catch a screening
At the Soho Hotel: I know. I'm lost. You can't
Get to the Soho Hotel down Beak Street but maybe
Today you can.

I'm dashing through Soho Square to find a voice studio
At the far end of Berwick Street. I know. Lost again.
Except maybe I'm not really lost. Maybe Soho
Moves when you do.

I'm turning and turning in a place
That relocates itself when you're not looking
That's gas or liquid, always shapeshifting,
Always pulling itself out of a hat.

I'm standing in a street I've never seen before
Because that's how it is in Soho. Streets move,
Squares circle themselves, and you may as well
Tear up the map!

the company has gradually renewed the street and its environs. Fashion retailers have been attracted back and the adjacent Kingsley Court has been developed as a hive of small workshops and retail outlets. The revival of Soho over the last ten to fifteen years has also mirrored the emergence of the gay community as an economic force. No longer seen as part of Soho's seedy side, the gay community is one of the indicators that Richard Florida uses in his 'Boho Index' to identify creative places. Today, the bars of Old Compton Street are thriving to such an extent that the street has to be closed to traffic in the evenings, and the 'Pink Pound' is driving the transformation of the area.

Soho remains an internationally important centre for creative industries, particularly film and television production. There are hundreds of companies employing many thousands of people in these sectors, including the British Board for Film Classification. Symbolic of their importance is Sohonet – a global private digital network linking companies in Soho with the main film studios in Britain and Hollywood. This is of an altogether different scale to the smallscale creative industries fostered by other creative quarters; important as these small companies are, they cannot match the global reach of the media sector in Soho.

Alongside all of this, the area retains a strong residential community, albeit one under considerable pressures. Soho remains ethnically diverse with traces of all of the groups that have come into the area over the years visible in its shops, restaurants and churches. Indeed the Soho Primary School on Great Windmill Street, a few doors from the Windmill Theatre, continues to serve Soho's children. The community has survived the decline of the area, but now ironically is under greater threat from its success. Rising prices are pushing up values and rents, squeezing out local communities. The street life that spills out onto the streets of the area can also make

Mainstream retailers in Carnaby Street (above) sit alongside independent boutiques in Kingley Court (right) while fashionable streets still look much as they must have done 150 years ago.

it a difficult place to live. The community is however being preserved in part by the Soho Housing Trust, which has been developing new family housing in the area.

Soho is therefore a precarious balance of different and sometimes conflicting activities. A consortium of local businesses launched the 'I Love Soho' Campaign in 2006 to bring business back to the area and the same year Westminster Council published the Soho Action Plan, drawn up in partnership with a range of local groups. These initiatives are not so much about regenerating the area, but keeping all of the diverse uses that make Soho what it is, in a state of happy equilibrium. When this balancing act is maintained – as it is currently in Soho - the result is the most extraordinarily diverse and exciting neighbourhood.

The three neighbourhoods are all good examples of the role of creative quarters in the revival of cities. They are all different and it is perhaps unfair to compare them to each other. Grainger Town is a worthy winner of The Great Neighbourhood Award. It is the greatest regeneration achievement given the transformation that has been wrought in the area and it is also the most beautiful. Soho and Temple Bar by comparison look shabby and chaotic, their streets are littered, and it is still possible to find graffiti and fly-posting. The irony is that this messiness and chaos is what tends to attract creative people. This is the dilemma for regeneration agencies seeking to promote creative quarters. By definition, they cannot be counter-culture if they are seen to be a corporate or public sector project. Like dads dancing at a wedding reception, no matter how hard they try, they are never going to be quite cool enough.

References

1. Florida Richard: Who's Your City: How the Creative Economy is making where to live the most important decision of your life, Random House 2008 and...

Florida Richard: The rise of the creative class ...and how its transforming work leisure community and everyday life – Basic Books 2004

Anthony Reddy

Regional Identity in Urbanism

In an era when globalisation is becoming an increasingly dominant part of our culture, regional identity is coming under threat. The international expansion of trade and production, financial, media and commodity markets undoubtedly delivers increased quality of service and goods in a more open and competitive economy. Throughout the world, however, people are induced to meet their needs not through the local economy but through the global market. Western societies have become increasingly similar to one another - and are becoming increasingly homogenised in the process.

Is there a danger that our towns and cities are becoming similarly homogenised? There is little doubt that post-war modernist planning, based on the principles of the Charter of Athens - segregation of the city through separate land use zoning and a dominant emphasis on car-based transport - have contributed to greater similarities. While most cities have their modernist interventions, with retail and commercial boxes in anonymous suburbs on the edge, there has been a growing recognition of the value of individual urban identity. Cities as diverse as London, Paris, Berlin, Copenhagen, St. Petersburg and Buenos Aires have engaged in urban regeneration and renewal programmes based on their unique character. This has led to a growing recognition among the citizens of these cities and their competitors of the value of a distinct urban identity. It is an irony that, in this era of globalisation, the uniqueness of regional urbanism and identity is becoming increasingly valued.

The most successful cities and towns have certain essential qualities, recognisable patterns and complexity that define their form. Throughout Europe, we find attractive cities and towns that are legible and therefore easier to negotiate. Whether it is cities like Barcelona, Edinburgh and Dublin or towns such

Naples

The views from the top of two Cathedrals illustrate the different characters of Barcelona (below) and Seville (right)

as Oxford, Kilkenny and Siena, we constantly experience this clear legibility particularly in the historical cores. They share other characteristics: mixed uses, people living in the town centre, sometimes above their place of work and a consistency of use of materials. Such cities and towns, whether their growth has been planned or they have developed organically, exhibit an order for the whole: blocks and streets, squares and courts that come together to form a dense and inter-related pattern of buildings and circulation routes. This produces an urban design context made up of a limited number of elements that form a larger whole in a variety of different ways, creating a unique identity.

The towns and cities that have evolved incrementally are often the best examples of regional identity in urbanism, with infinite variations from country to country and region to region. The network of streets represents the structure that defines the fabric of a city's urbanism: the close grain in the town centres, a wider grain in the suburbs. The city block is the original cell of each urban structure, and the tighter its grain, the more legible and permeable is the town or city. It defines the networks of routes around its edges and within its boundaries it creates a unique plot structure. There is also a variety of scale and an overlying hierarchy in the arrangement of

the main uses and communication networks, with flexibility to move these uses. A combination of a tight and loose fit, the urban texture is dense enough to provide short walking distances so that pedestrians can move easily and in comfort from one place to another.

Cities and towns have been laboratories for testing urbanism theories for centuries. Religious leaders such as Pope Sixtus V had a major impact on sixteenth-century Rome. Philip II of Spain determined the future form of most central and south American cities with his Law of the Indies. Haussmann's Paris and Cerdà's Barcelona are prime examples of mid-nineteenth century planning initiatives. However, cities are built by all sorts of people, from the medieval lords of England, France or Spain who planted hundreds of new towns within their territories; military engineers who laid out the ports and cities of the British, French and Dutch empires; administrators and state officials, down to the modern city planners.

European cities and towns have a common history from the Renaissance, Reformation and Enlightenment to 1914, 1945 and 1989. While different parts of Europe have had a greater or lesser involvement in these historical events, this is reflected in their urbanism. The Roman Empire left its mark on the figure ground plan of most cities within its borders. Non-Roman towns had a less rigorous yet no less legible form.

Throughout history, the urban form of our cities and towns has been legislated in ways that reflect contemporary society. The admired example of medieval Siena had a premeditated form that determined the use of special materials and even defined the size and shape of doors and windows. The historical circumstances of Siena's origin and growth influenced its city form and led to a particular form of medieval urbanism.

The planning of Haussmann's Paris was a large-scale initiative that also determined precise standards for the smallest of details – the heights of eaves lines, pilasters, balconies and corbelling. In Barcelona, Ildefons Cerdà designed a plan for the Eixample (extension) in 1864 consisting of a grid of streets and perimeter blocks covering an area of nine square kilometres (see page 15). Consisting of 113.3 square metre blocks with chamfered corners and streets that are 20 metres wide, this vast area has become, with its counterpoint to the medieval city, part of Barcelona's unique identity in spite of being imposed in the first instance by the Government from Madrid. From the outset, it has absorbed a range of architectural styles from the modernism of Domenech i Montaner to the individualism of Gaudí. The Cerdà plan has continued to influence Barcelona's urban form, while - for the people of this city - the urban architectural character remains synonymous with being Catalan.

By contrast, the chaos of London, the piling up of a variety of building styles with limited planning, constitutes a political statement: an act of defiance against the absolute power of a ruler, against a bureaucracy, against Wren's version of Haussmann or Cerdà.

Edinburgh's Old Town sited on the tail of the Castle Rock was originally home to Scotland's royalty and parliament and a population which lived at a density of 700 per acre, mixing classes and trades. The Georgian New Town was an attempt to attract aristocrats back to the city, and the inhabitants of the New Town introduced planning regulations to ensure that their 'genteel and well-ordered arcady' was not compromised.

Sweden went through the same phases of industrialisation as many other European countries, but there has always been a latent nostalgia for their rural background among Swedes. For over 80 years, the cool logic of social democracy has been dominant and is evident throughout Stockholm. Outlying neighbourhoods with their broad lanes and large leafy courtyards exhibit a social concern – a tradition continued in the recent regeneration project at Hammarby – one of Europe's best examples of sustainable urbanism.

Madrid has an extraordinary vitality and sense of scale - from the exhilarating granite heights of the Sierra de Guadarrama to the expanse of sun-scorched high-rise housing that rises abruptly from an ochre backdrop. Despite extensive rebuilding in the aftermath of the Spanish civil war, certain districts retain much of the character of the period when they were first built. The Plaza de la Paja had been the palace-lined main square of the medieval town. On the other hand, the Paseo de la Castellana accommodates recent examples of Spanish architecture consisting of longer city blocks and culminating in modern towers.

Helsinki's position on an exposed cape is largely responsible for the city's most characteristic contrasts and intensively urban older town, with suburbs set in natural woodland surroundings where the forest landscape of central Finland comes right into the heart of the city. Public transportation accounts for a high proportion of workgenerated trips, contrasting with a dispersed regional pattern based on private car use.

In England and Ireland, the form of domestic architecture had a profound influence on the way the city was perceived. The repetitious nature of the speculatively built terrace house came to dominate most English and Irish cities including London,

Hammarby Sjöstad in Stockholm

Dublin, Bath and Bristol. This uniformity and simplicity of design and the predominant use of brick, created a fine grain that was a defining image of these cities until the early part of the twentieth century.

The tenement apartment building is an ubiquitous European building typology. It is the prototypical residence for city dwellers of all social classes. The tenements of Scotland's cities proclaim that country's historically close European ties leaving a continuing tradition of apartment living in their urban cores and suburbs for all classes.

The legal and economic history that affects city-making is an enormous subject. It involves ownership of urban land and the property market: the relative power of government to take over private property for public use; the institution of the legally binding masterplan, the piano regolatore of the Italians; the building codes and other regulatory systems; instruments of funding urban change, like property taxes and bond issues; and the administrative structure of cities.

Cities and towns are amalgams of buildings and people. They are inhabited settings from which daily actions from the minor to the important, the random to the organised, derive their validity. In the city and town is the ultimate memory of humanity's struggles and efforts; it is where pride in the past is put on display. Sometimes cities and towns are laid out by order, as geometrical shapes, or for specific purposes. Sometimes they may aim to reflect some higher order or ideal society, or be prepared to assist as an area of defence at a time of war, or have no more important purpose than to be a place to generate business. But whether founded under religious guidance or speculative drive, the pattern will fail unless the people within it forge a self-sustaining life that can survive adversity and changes of fortune.

The origins of many cities and towns is humble and the evolution of their form gradual. Where once there were fields and pastoral land, streets materialised and linked up to public places to engage public life as the spread of buildings thickened and meshed, following the slopes and bends of the terrain. In time, these natural arrangements came to suggest institutional and social hierarchies. The winding street made way for visual delights, encompassing more formal elements and intricacies, and we expect adventurous city-makers to recreate these effects. The picturesque suburb is the city's retrospective celebration of its natural origin. This belief has sustained nostalgia for the irregularities of townscape and organic patterns that once ensured social cohesion. But in many cases the sense of community sought has been reduced by the effects of road systems on engineering principles.

Much of the suburban development in European towns and cities in the post-war period is bereft of character when compared with the places we regard as models of good urban design – the historic cores of our major cities and towns and established residential areas. However, while we admire such places, we consistently build something very different – the familiar sprawl of modern suburbia.

Our planning standards, as articulated in most development plans, facilitate – indeed encourage – segmented growth, which actually makes it impossible to incorporate the urban design qualities we associate with existing towns and their hierarchy of public spaces.

We live in an age of public concern for the built environment, yet we are only beginning to grapple with what is essential in the art of town and city-making. On the one hand, our planning systems seem mired in the bureaucratic realm of policy formulation and macro-economic issues, unrelated to the spatial dimension of communities. On the other hand, architects and concerned members of the public are consumed by detail and image. Consequently, we continue to build vast tracts of repetitive developments that do not form neighbourhoods, towns or cities.

London is defined by the townhouse

The Interwar suburb is what has come to dominate many English towns and cities

Many architects and town planners prefer to ignore the suburb, hoping that it will prove to be as inconsequential as it is distasteful. Most built environment professionals think of themselves as urbanists who appreciate the value of cities and towns where culture and civic space interact naturally. Because of this, we consider the city and urban values to be dominant in our culture and the suburbs as an aberrant form of settlement. However, the reality is that in Britain and Ireland, as in most western countries, the suburb is the predominant form of settlement.

The suburbs also have a persuasive hold on the imagination of most citizens and, unless we confront that fact, suburban norms will continue to dominate urban forms. Refusing to recognise the impact of the Edge City phenomenon – the new linear areas developing along motorways and the fringes of cities and towns – while concentrating our efforts on model inner city renewal projects is unlikely to provide the solutions that are needed for contemporary urbanism.

The various forms of suburban development reflect differences in local culture, banking systems, transport, building technique and administrative authority. The spectrum of suburban residential development spans two poles: from the patchwork of detached and semi-detached houses at one extreme to the juxtaposition of apartment and tenement blocks at the other. These opposite settlement patterns are also aligned to the extremes of laissez-faire as opposed to centrally planned systems.

In Britain and Ireland, our cities and towns are spreading out at an alarming rate, influenced by a North American approach to urbanism rather than sustainable models. This form of settlement, with its emphasis on mobility by car and the preference for privacy over sociability, has potentially serious consequences for the future of our cities and towns.

The suburbs are too deeply embedded in our psyche to disappear as a phenomenon. It is a challenge facing European architects and urbanists in the 21st century to tackle and control this dominant form of settlement. The pressure to provide new homes in growing cities and towns will not decrease. Accordingly, we can anticipate that the regeneration and extension of our towns and spaces will continue to be a dominant theme in the 21st century.

There is a growing recognition within society that the patterns of town expansion of the past half-century are not appropriate if we are to achieve a sustainable environment. In the future, we must meet demand by building places based on the principles of an appropriate masterplan or framework plan, respecting local character, creating distinctive form and place, while achieving better densities and layouts and a high quality public realm.

A fundamental principle of 21st century urbanism is that places matter more than buildings and roads. In addition, urbanists should accept that what has succeeded in the past can usefully inform the way we design and manage new, innovative environments.

The pre-industrial city that is compact, dense, layered and slow-changing has a particular hold on public perception. In the post-war period, most European cities and towns underwent unprecedented change in the form of their built environment and transportation systems. There was a general emphasis on making provision for the motor car that had a negative impact on urban form, resulting in much of the soulless edge cities, banlieues and barrios. More recently, however, there has been recognition that high-quality public transportation has provided excellent integration into the street network. Amsterdam, Bordeaux, Dublin, Strasbourg and Lisbon demonstrate how new public transport systems can be catalysts for urban regeneration.

In a society where privatisation is in the ascendant, many cities and towns have effectively turned over the decisions on their future form to developers, private companies and their architects and planners. The interest of the community is not necessarily the same as those of the developers and private interests. The planning and vision for many of our modern cities and towns, like other negotiated settings of our past, cannot be assessed on economic and aesthetic grounds alone. It is the balance between private interest and public good, supervised by the citizenry, that has traditionally produced the most memorable cities and towns. The aesthetics and vision of how cities and towns will look should be provided by creative and sympathetic architects and urban designers. The local authorities and their advisers should find planning solutions to the problem of laissez-faire growth. But it is the citizens, as a collective group, who must ultimately decide the shape of the cities and towns. Like the communes of Tuscany which took charge of city form in the late Middle Ages and shaped it to reflect their governance and political and social priorities, so it should be in the modern age for us.

Our cities and towns are amongst the most complicated and wondrous artefacts that man has created. In addition, they are the cumulative generational entities that express our values as a community and provide us with the setting where we can live together. Accordingly, it is our collective responsibility to guide their design in appropriate fashion.

One of the most prevalent reasons for the existence of cities and towns has been exchange. Trade, manufacturing and service activities have been the central economic concern through history.

Economic growth has changed much of the older fabric of our cities and towns. New development has often been carried out without appropriate regard for quality and material. Such developments form neither good nor urban places because they erode the urban grain and texture.

Globalisation is both a threat and an opportunity for our cities and towns, particularly those that are not world cities. There is a danger that as cities pursue ideas of individuality and distinctiveness they will create places, spaces and buildings of the same type and appearance. However, this will make original urban places and spaces that sustain a physical and urban identity the centrepieces of successful cities and towns in the 21st century.

During the Renaissance, city-states such as Venice, Florence and Milan competed with each other to achieve high standards in architecture and urbanism. In a united Europe, where the importance of the nation state is in decline, there is increasing evidence of competition among cities and regions to attract inward investment.

As the great urbanist Jane Jacobs pointed out, successful places are multidimensional and diverse, full of creativity and stimulation. Her seminal work, The Death and Life of Great American Cities, celebrated the creativity and diversity of urban neighbourhoods such as Greenwich Village. Jacobs' neighbourhoods, such as Hudson Street, were centres of individuality, difference and social interaction. The neighbourhood street where many different kinds of people came together was both a source of civility and a centre of creativity.

There is now a wider recognition and appreciation of the principles which Jacobs exposed. Urban neighbourhoods similar to Hudson Street are renewing throughout the world and many of the principles that animated it are diffusing in different cities and societies.

For the future, those cities and towns that appreciate and protect their urban cores while promoting sustainable interventions and extensions are the ones most likely to succeed. The challenge for architects, urban designers, planners, policymakers, legislators and all those involved in the future of our cities and towns is to recognise the importance of regional identity to quality urbanism and identity in a globalised world, and to enhance opportunities for preservation and intervention in maintaining and creating sustainable mixed-use communities.

References:
Spiro Kostof: The City Assembled and The Elements of Urban Form through History, Thames and Hudson, London 1992
Richard Florida: The Rise of the Creative Class, Basic Books, New York 2002
Kevin Lynch: Good City Form, Thames and Hudson, London 1992
Fridrib Banjergee and **Michael Southbank:** City Sense and City Design – Writings and Projects of Kevin Lynch, MIT Press, Cambridge, MA 1990
Peter Hall: Cities of Civilisation: Culture Technology and Urban Order 1998, Weidenfeld and Nicolson, London 1998
Jane Jacobs: Cities and the Wealth of Nations, Random House, 1984
Jane Jacobs: The Death and Life of the Great American Cities, Vintage Books, 1961

Frank McDonald

Great Streets: Thoroughfares of Urbanism

Buchanan Street, Regent Street & O'Connell Street

Three great streets, O'Connell Street (top), Regent Street (middle) and Buchanan Street (bottom)

There's a colourful framed poster in my study that says "PEO-PLE LIVE HERE - SAVE OUR STREETS". It's a relic from the late 1980s when we were protesting against dastardly plans by Dublin Corporation's road engineers to level terraces of historic buildings in the city to make room for dual-carriageways carrying traffic into town from the suburbs. For those involved in this campaign, it was a do-or-die struggle to save the city and, though we didn't win every battle, we eventually won the war - or, at least, the central argument that streets are primarily places for people, and not merely thoroughfares.

From the 1960s onwards, nearly every city made compromises to cater for traffic; that was the thesis of the time. But times have changed, and most cities in Europe are now trying to tame traffic, rather than cater for it. Pedestrians, cyclists, buses, trams and taxis are being given more and more space, as a result of conscious political choices informed by visions of making the city more civilised. Anyone who doubts this should go to Bordeaux and see how its new tramway has helped to transform the city; its honey-coloured sandstone buildings are gleaming now and the main public spaces filled with people.

Only one of the three Great Street Award nominees, Buchanan Street in Glasgow, currently enjoys an equivalent level of civility. Traffic still trundles through the other two, O'Connell Street in Dublin and Regent Street in London, but this will change in time. What the three share, however, is a determination by key stakeholders to improve the public realm - led by enlightened civic leadership. In all three cases, there is also a recognition of the importance of these streets as elements in the 'city brand' and of the need to ensure that projected images are matched by the reality on the ground, particularly for visitors.

O'Connell Street

Unlike Buchanan Street and Regent Street, O'Connell Street is a grand boulevard. One of the most impressive main streets in Europe, it is 500 metres long and 46 metres wide, with statues of Irish historical figures lined up on the central median - most notably, sculptor John Henry Foley's tribute to The Liberator Daniel O'Connell, surrounded by a retinue of four angels at the southern end of the street, and Augustus Saint-Gaudens' monument to Charles Stewart Parnell, the 'uncrowned king of Ireland', at its northern end.

Laid out in the mid-18th century as Sackville Mall (named after the then Lord Lieutenant of Ireland, Lionel Cranfield Sackville, Duke of Dorset), it became O'Connell Street in 1882. For more than 150 years, until it was blown up by the IRA in 1966, its centrepiece was Nelson Pillar, a huge Doric column that rose to a height of 120 feet (36 metres). In its place today stands the Dublin Spire, a 120-metre stainless steel needle by Ian Ritchie. More contemptuously known by cynics as 'The Spike' or 'The Stiletto in the Ghetto', it has become a symbol of the rejuvenation of the street in recent years, after decades of being down at heel, with wider pavements on each side and a central plaza in front of the historic General Post Office.

It was at the GPO, on Easter Monday 1916, that Padraig Pearse proclaimed the Irish Republic. The rebellion he led was crushed by the Crown forces after a week of fierce fighting, during which the GPO was shelled from a British gunboat in the River Liffey. The building, with its hexastyle Ionic portico, was reduced to a roofless ruin and much of the west side of the street destroyed. After the foundation of the Irish Free State in 1921, a bitter civil war broke out, leading to the destruction of much of the east side of the street. Not only did the new Irish Government restore the GPO, but most of the street was rebuilt in grand neoclassical style in the 1920s under the direction of then City Architect Horace Tennyson O'Rourke. Notable buildings include the Gresham Hotel and Clery's department store, which was modelled on Selfridge's in London.

The heyday of O'Connell Street was in the 1950s, with popular places of entertainment such as Metropole and Clery's Ballroom as well as the Capitol, Carlton and Savoy cinemas, Cafolla and Palm Grove ice cream parlours, and the often glittering social life that centred on the Gresham. But the destruction of Nelson Pillar symbolically ushered in a long period of decline as Dublin society, and even the city's centre of gravity, moved south of the river. The Metropole and Capitol closed as did the Carlton and the ice cream parlours, and it was taken over by amuse-

The life of O'Connell Street

ment arcades and burger joints; in fact, they were among the few prepared to invest in the street.

Various efforts were made to find a suitable replacement for The Pillar, as everyone called it, but it was not until 1998 when Dublin City Council produced an integrated area plan for O'Connell Street that its fortunes began to change, heralded by a radical re-ordering of the public domain. An international design competition for the Pillar site ushered in the new era. It attracted over 200 entries, ranging from an enormous tattered Tricolour seemingly shot through by machinegun-fire to a 'Love Elevator' featuring the romantic musings of Irish poets. Ian Ritchie's secular spire was hugely controversial, generating heated debate in the letters pages of the Irish Times. However, a large crowd gathered in O'Connell Street to watch it being capped in 2003, bursting into spontaneous applause, and it quickly became a symbol of the city and used to form the 'I' in Dublin.

Lime trees, pleached in the French manner, were planted to form a square in front of the GPO, paved in high-quality granite and limestone, following the example of the Champs-Élysées in Paris, while the old London planes that used to dominate the street were replaced with regrettably ill-chosen mountain ash and silver birch. Pedestrians could barely believe the generosity of space being given to them, as footpaths on both sides of the street were doubled in width, though the needs of cyclists for their own narrow lanes were only provided for as an afterthought. Much of the traffic now consists of double-deck buses and the street is also crossed by the Luas trams running from Tallaght to Connolly Station.

There is a particularly heavy footfall at the Spire, mainly shoppers crossing between North Earl Street and Henry Street, one of Dublin's principal shopping areas. But a magnet is needed to draw them north of this east-west axis, bringing more life to Upper O'Connell Street, and the most likely is a shopping centre scheme for the

O'Connell Street signs and (above) The Spire, designed by Ian Richie Architects

O'CONNELL STREET, DUBLIN

Wide street. Wide street, this.
Widest street you've walked down today.
Street so unbelievably, astonishingly wide
It takes yesterday and tomorrow in its gargantuan stride.

Widest street in Ireland, this. Wide street.
Wide bridge. Wider than it's long. So wide
You can keep history and culture deep inside
As you walk and walk and the dance moves your feet.

Wide. Widest street in Ireland. Widest street
In Europe, if not the World. Say 'I'll meet
You on O'Connell Street' and they have to bring a map
Or sandwiches as they walk slowly across...

Widest street in Dublin. Widest Street in Ireland.
Widest street in Europe. Widest street in the World.
As O'Connell Street is unrolled and unfurled
I can walk across it to the Moon. And beyond.

O'Connell Street figure ground plan

Carlton site and adjoining properties. The City Council had to acquire this critical site by compulsory purchase following the failure of earlier plans to redevelop it and, after much legal wrangling, a five-acre site is now controlled by property developer Chartered Land. The latest plan - drawn up by architects BKD, Donnelly Turpin and McGarry NíÉanaigh - would create two new streets to link O'Connell Street with both Moore Street and Henry Street, to the west and south respectively, and would include a cascading high-rise apartment block topped by a slanting 'park in the sky' with an unfortunate north-easterly orientation.

Another major shopping precinct is due to be installed along Princes Street, on the southern side of the GPO, when Arnott's department store extends into the former Independent Newspapers offices and printing works. But whether O'Connell Street can absorb so much additional retail is doubtful. Meanwhile, the former Ambassador cinema - built as a moneyraising concert hall in the mid-18th century as part of the Rotunda maternity hospital on Parnell Square - is to be converted into a new central library for the city, replacing a makeshift facility located in the ILAC shopping centre on Moore Street. It will form part of a wider vision of turning Parnell Square into a new cultural zone, which also includes the Gate Theatre and the recently extended Hugh Lane Dublin City Gallery. The Garden of Remembrance, commemorating Ireland's freedom struggle, is also being opened up while a 1916 museum is planned for the GPO. Plans for a metro line linking Dublin Airport with St. Stephen's Green have been amended to include an underground station on the east side of Parnell Square, and it seem likely that this - together with the other planned developments - will finally lift Upper O'Connell Street.

Regent Street

London's Regent Street also needs a lift, though not quite in the same way. Defined by its famous curve, as designed by John Nash, it is one of the main north-south routes through the West End and carries a significant level of traffic. Few realise that most of the buildings are post-Edwardian, rather than Regency, following an extensive rebuilding in the 1920s when the original leases were up for renewal; the only work by Nash that survives is All Souls Church. Another important fact not widely known outside London is that Regent Street is part of the Crown Estate, which started buying land in this part of the city as long ago as 1670 and still owns freehold title to all of the properties there.

Regent Street

Originally designed as a shopping and commercial street, Regent Street was developed in the 19th century and redeveloped in the 20th century. This was done on head leases from the Crown Estate, which merely laid down specifications for façades, and these could cover up anything. So essentially, it's a stage set. Ownership gave the estate "all the responsibility, but no power", said David Shaw, its head of strategy and development, and he was determined to change this balance, "With the head leases beginning to expire, we decided that the key thing was to get control, so that we could drive the whole process ourselves and so far we've done ten schemes."

Located between Regent's Park and St. James's Park, Portland Place and Regent Street run for a distance of 3km. Portland Place, designed by Robert Adam, still has most of its original buildings as well as the opulent Langham Hotel (1856), which is said to be Europe's first real 'grand hotel'. All Souls, the only intact Nash church in London, stands at the head of Regent Street with the BBC's new extension looming up behind it. The BBC is investing heavily in transforming the world's first purpose-built Broadcasting House into a digital broadcasting centre. "It's about re-inventing the past for the future", according to the BBC's Robert Seatter. "One of our key aspirations is to create new

public spaces, so there will be a World Piazza here by 2012".

The other 'event' is Piccadilly Circus, where Regent Street cranks to run south to Waterloo Place, offering a superb view of the Houses of Parliament at Westminster - albeit from behind ghastly sheep-pen railings, intended to keep pedestrians in their place. The aim is to get rid of these obstructions and transform the lower end of the street from what Shaw describes as a "pretty poor car park" into a place for people. There is already an annual 'VIP Day' - VIP meaning Very Important Pedestrian, and an annual festival every autumn; in 2006, it had a Spanish theme and in 2007 it was Indian. Places for eating such as Heddon Street are also being encouraged, with traffic banned from accessing it at lunchtime to allow outdoor tables to spill into the street, as in Barcelona or Paris.

Views of Regent Street including the Christmas Lights (opposite), Broadcasting House (top left) and the Quadrant Arcade (below left)

Regent Street's slogan, 'Where time is always well spent', relates mainly to shopping. In the past, the retail offer wasn't particularly good, but it has been lifted by flagship stores such as Aquascutum, Burberry, Hamleys and Jaeger, as well as a very busy Apple store. With forty-five new retailers brought in since 2002, there is now a better and more varied retail mix, and this makes the street much more attractive. The four benchmarks used by the Crown Estate in selecting retailers are 'quality, heritage, style and success' - and aspirants who don't fit these criteria are rejected. "We turn down people quite regularly", Shaw said. "As with shopping centres, someone has to decide. We're not a mass market big pedestrian footfall street, though of course the pay-off for developing it would be higher rents, so its partly a commercial strategy".

One of the Crown Estate's more important schemes involves the former Regent Palace Hotel on Glasshouse Street, off Piccadilly Circus. With the exception of its corner pavilions, it was to be demolished to make way for a mixed use residential, office and retail development. It is in these side streets, as architect Peter Heath explained, that you can see "the interface between the grand conception and the narrow grain", often with the effect of turning the side streets into mere service areas. So one of the objectives here is to "keep them clear of clutter". Glasshouse Street is being re-paved in a big diamond pattern of granite setts and York stone, designed by Jeremy Dixon. However, the Regent Palace hotel use will be replaced by a new five-star hotel in the Café Royal building, which is currently often used for auctions.

The Crown Estate has been taking a very pro-active approach to improvements in the public realm – a team effort that involves other stakeholders in the area such as the BBC, the City of Westminster, the New West End Company and the Regent Street Association. The New West End Company, incidentally, runs the biggest BID (business improvement district) in Britain, covering Regent Street, Bond Street and Oxford Street, with a budget of £6 million - half of it raised from the business community and half from the Mayor of London. "One of our successes has been to get so many public and private organisations on the same wavelength", said Shaw, who is the company's deputy chairman. "You can invest as much as you like in buildings, but unless you do something about the space between them, it's a waste of time." Ultimately, they are working towards realising Sir Terry Farrell's vision of creating a walkable boulevard, or 'Nash Ramblas'.

Regent Street figure ground plan

REGENT STREET/PORTLAND PLACE , LONDON

You walk this dream called Regent Street;
 You look at the maps and digest the plans
And you feel that London is somehow completed
By Portland Place and Regent Street.

This street's an idea moved from paper to stone
 To reflected light and wall-wafted sound
And then to a prism of angle and tone:
Portland Place stone, Regent Street stone.

Stroll down this vision of what strolling could be:
A drifting meander to the heart of the city
With senses alive as you hear, smell, touch, see:
A taste of how things could be...

The crowds of Buchanan Street

Buchanan Street

Buchanan Street in Glasgow doesn't have the climate to become anything like the original Ramblas; practically the only trait it shares with Barcelona's best-known street (and with both O'Connell Street and Regent Street) is a north-south orientation. As Brian Evans, partner in Glasgow-based Gillespies landscape architects, who played a major role in reshaping the street noted, "Buchanan Street is the city's spine, so the first important thing is not to break it". As part of Glasgow's famous grid, Buchanan Street, which runs downhill from the Royal Concert Hall to St. Enoch's Square, is the 'hinge' between the city's first and second new towns. Pedestrianised in 1978, the up-grading of its public realm was completed in 2001.

Much of the city's recent transformation derives from the 'Glasgow can do it' slogan devised by the City Council and Scottish Development Agency - then headed by Stuart Gulliver - after they got together to form Glasgow Action in the late 1980s. Glasgow city centre was crying out for attention and needed to be made more attractive to business, inward investment and as a place to live. It could only benefit from an effort to 'benchmark' the city against European competitors, such as Amsterdam. In that context, Buchanan Street - 1km long and just over 20 metres wide - was identified as Glasgow's 'front door', rather than the more formal civic space of George Square. But a lot of work needed to be done to improve its public realm and public life. Gillespies with MBM, from Barcelona, looked at where people were coming from and going to, with a view to overcoming issues of access and circulation - based on an understanding of the topography of the city and the way people used its streets.

Some of the projects that flowed from this 'communication and consultation' exercise include the net of celestial light over Royal Exchange Square - the 'Christmas duvet', as some call it - and the radical departure of throwing blue light on Buchanan Street. New street lamps, placed using the golden section, were installed all the way along the street, with cafés on the east side catching the afternoon and evening sun. Provision was also made for canopied enclosures, such as Rogano's restaurant, so people could eat outdoors. Street furniture includes solid blocks of highly polished stone seats. The street is lined mainly by 19th century commercial buildings and includes the Princes Square shopping mall. Traffic is restricted to two crossings, at St. Vincent Street and Nelson Mandela Place. Formerly St.

BUCHANAN STREET, GLASGOW

My dad would talk about Buchanan Street,
About the excitement of it, for a small-town lad
From Lanarkshire. 'It moved like a river' he said once,
And I've never forgotten that.

Well, dad, come and see it now, old warrior,
See how the river runs! Then remember
That old story about if you look at a river one day,
Then look at it tomorrow, it's not the same river.

You can never see the same river twice, dad.
Buchanan Street flows and changes all the time,
Never the same street twice, always moving,
Always splashing and always returning.

Buchanan Street is a river, Dad. Come and sail.

Buchanan Street figure ground plan

George's Place, it was renamed by the City Council after the famous South African statesman when he was still imprisoned in Robben Island and when the Apartheid regime's Scottish Consulate was located there – the Consulate relocated. The refurbishment scheme also included reconfiguring the city's underground stations, with new canopies and station entrances to make the experience of using it more like air travel - before all of the hassles necessitated by heightened security requirements at airports.

The jewel in Glasgow's public realm requires to be cleaned to keep it sparkling

Buchanan Street is covered by Glasgow City Council's Safer City Centre initiative, which involves working with the police, health board and business community. Its aim, according to city centre task force co-ordinator Willie Caie, is to 'make sure people enjoy themselves'. Some two hundred businesses work together in partnership with dedicated patrols, community police and radio links from shops to the CCTV control centre, which monitors ninety cameras in the city centre as well as two CCTV vehicles. It was recently extended to include nightclubs. With over five hundred licensed premises in central Glasgow, there are lots of people on the street day and night, particularly at weekends. The capacity of nightclubs alone is fifty thousand. Bus and taxi marshals have been deployed, and upgraded lighting installed in the 'night zone'.

On Buchanan Street, as elsewhere in the city centre, new triple-tiered planters with attractive floral displays are part of a beautification programme to support Glasgow's successful bid for the 2014 Commonwealth Games. It also benefits from the Clean Glasgow initiative. Hugh McKergow, the Council's head of cleansing operations, described the street as "the jewel in Glasgow's public realm", though he quickly added that it "requires to be cleaned to keep it sparkling". Special low pressure, high-temperature washing treatment is used on its Caithness stone and granite. The machine is "practically noiseless" because its diesel engine is insulated. Chewing gum is mechanically removed as part of a £400,000 city-wide programme. Eight to ten tonnes of waste is 'lifted' every day, mostly from shops, after the 10am deadline for deliveries. Stainless steel litterbins, originally provided as part of the public realm improvements, had to be replaced by more robust cast-iron ones because their doors fell off and they were "not easy to empty", McKergow told us. New litter bins, in a better design, are coming in.

Rather surprisingly for a street that does so much business, there is an ugly derelict site at its northern end, opposite the stone-faced Buchanan Galleries - a 600,000 sq ft shopping centre, which was designed in the early 1990s and is due to be reno-

vated and extended. Tom Murray, of BDP, said their Buchanan Quarter Development Framework would aim to ameliorate the "very inward-looking shopping centre" (aren't they all?) and make the front of the Royal Concert Hall, which reads almost like an adjunct to the centre, "more visually open". At the southern end of Buchanan Street, architects Cooper Cromar are re-modelling St. Enoch's Square shopping centre by creating a new 'entrance box' on the corner and stonefaced elevation to the square, which will have cafés spilling out onto a re-paved area.

With so much retail space, the Lonely Planet guide described Glasgow as a 'shopaholic's paradise'. David Ross, of Glasgow Chamber of Commerce, says retail is worth a staggering £4.5 billion per annum to the city's economy and is part of Glasgow's success as a 'city brand'. Along with the variety of the Merchant City, which won the Academy's first Great Neighbourhood Award, Buchanan Street projects quite a different image of the 'new Glasgow' than, say, the Gorbals or the M8 motorway, which looks like it was driven through the city as sensitively as someone hacking his way through the jungle with a machete. It is clear, however, that Buchanan Street is cherished and valued - and rightly celebrated by the Academy's Great Street Award. Yet another feather in Glasgow's cap.

Frank Walker

Identity at the Edge

"No building of distinction in the past or the present has been created by a conscious attempt to imbue architecture with a national characteristic" *G. Robertson, 1995*

In the beginning of the 21st century, commentators are addressing themselves more and more to an issue that seems to pre-occupy many in the Celtic nations. An issue once described by Nikolaus Pevsner, for example, as 'the Scottishness of Scottish architecture'. The topic is endlessly debated. Robertson and his ilk are entitled to their opinions, but they are far from accurate. In arguing the case, however, let us not get hung up on the dangerous ambiguities inherent in the meanings or connotations of the word 'national' - 'regional' or 'contextual' will do every bit as well. Ethnicity is an irrelevance here.

Nor does this essayist have any desire to become sidetracked by quibbling over just what might be meant by a 'building of distinction'. In fact, the criteria used to form our judgements of quality can easily be constructed to suit our purposes. Furthermore, in arguing against Robertson's quasi-internationalist quote above, it should be clear that there is no necessary correlation between regionalist design and good architecture. But the view that no good architecture ever emerged from a consciously national or regional programme is both a misreading of architectural history and, more alarmingly, an abdication of cultural obligation and responsibility. Given the time and the space it would be a relatively straightforward matter to substantiate the creative legacy of the regionalist imperative from 15th century Brunelleschi to 20th century Botta.

The essay is entitled 'identity at the edge' because we are now at a historical edge. The beginning of a new century, indeed of a millennium – how quickly our preocccupation with that word vanished as we progressed through the

Is there something Scottish about the architecture of Edinburgh?

Is there a spirit of place in the Scottish Parliament Building by the Spanish Architect Enric Miralles?

'noughties'. Of course, there is no reason to expect that the year 2010, 2012 or even 2014 will be any more historically significant than, say, 1918, 1945 or 1984. Yet we cannot escape the almost mystical magic of the millennial effect, and we seem to be compelled to take stock of our place in time as we stand in this historical edge. As we do, we become more and more conscious of that place. Furthermore, Scotland and Ireland and England for the matter are also at a geographical edge - at the periphery of Europe.

What can we say about architecture at the edge? For example Scotland's architectural identity cannot but be affected by a sharpening consciousness of where we are in time and place. We are bound to locate ourselves somewhere in the context of the history of art, and architecture, and somewhere in the context of what Pevsner called 'the geography of art'. There is in short the 'spirit of the age' and the 'spirit of place', zeitgeist and genius loci, whose interplay determines cultural specificity.

As far as the 'spirit of the age' is concerned, we live in a post-modernist world. It is some time since Kenneth Frampton wrote his essay 'Modern Architecture and the Critical Present', but the situation is still largely as he described it - a fractured, pluralist spectrum of optional 'isms'. It is not that modernism has necessarily been rejected (although for some this is the case), but rather that particular aspects of the modernist ethos have achieved a kind of de facto independence under the leadership of various talented exponents.

As for the 'spirit of place', the experience in Scotland is somewhat raw and peripheral. It is not any ethnic edge that cuts into our psyche, for this is blunted by the lack of any strong linguistic frontiers, but a primordial geographical edge. Beyond us is the ocean. After Scotland or Ireland, the traveller falls off Europe into the abyss. Culturally speaking, we are at the existential edge that sharpens self-awareness in a special way. As one 19th century writer, David Masson, put it, the Scotsman's 'walk as a thinker, is not by the meadows and wheatfields, and the green lanes, and the ivy-clad parish churches, where all is gentle and antique and fertile, but by the bleak seashore which parts the certain from the limitless, where there is doubt in the seamews' shriek, and where it is well if, in the advancing tide, he can find a footing on a rock'.

Britain and Ireland's peripheral position and perspective have honed our cultural experience in an equally unique way. The great movements in European art, the tidal surges in cultural history have taken longer to reach our shores, becoming diluted, diffused or discontinuous in their wash across the britannic rocks. Yet, by virtue of our relative remoteness, we have developed a distinctive culture. For much of the time Scotland and Ireland have been intimately engaged with their immediate neighbour, England - economically, politically and culturally.

Some 20 years ago, Paul Scott paraphrased Pierre Trudeau when he described Scotland's relationship with England like being 'in bed with an elephant' in a Saltire Society essay. To escape this single powerful relationship, the Celtic nations have developed or been conditioned by other European ties. After all, as Kevin Lynch might put it – an edge is a path too; and the Scots and the Irish have repeatedly found paths around England - some Franco-Celtic and some Norse-Baltic.

No design is solely national or regional. There is virtually no Scottish architecture that was not first imported from another country. 'The architecture of Scotland is chiefly of foreign origin. But the richly turreted chateau and the church of flamboyant Gothic, when transported from France to our own rugged shores and sterile moorland, adapted themselves, under the hands of our ancestors, to the necessities of their new position, and underwent a series of changes which were better suited to the available materials, to the climate, and to the tastes and habits and wants (and, one might add, the expectations) of the people of Scotland' wrote Inglis in 1868.

So this is not a polemic for an introverted, narrow-visioned regional architecture of updated brochs and blackhouses. But a valid architecture, a distinctly Scottish architecture, must give form to the recurrent dialectic between the history - and geography - of art and architecture. If it is true that we can not be validly national without being in touch with the international, then we cannot be international without having something national to contribute. We cannot escape history, because history is now. We cannot escape geography, because geography is here. And here and now, at the edge of the century and the continent, the English, the Scots, the Welsh and the Irish are faced with a cultural choice.

This interaction between the more or less constant qualities imparted by the geography of art and the changing influences flooding over these islands in the course of the history of art is a continuing experience. It is this that impels and enriches our aesthetic expression. For example, despite its international ubiquity in the 18th century, Classicism in Scotland did become distinctly Scottish. Or again, amongst its internationally indiscriminate expressions through the 19th century, historicism did put on a recognisably Scottish face. But what is interesting is that the keenness of this dialectic increased towards the moment when centuries turn - when identity, both historical and geographical, somehow seemed to need sharpening – as when culture was very much 'at the edge'. In the late 18th century, as ideas and events moved Classicism towards Romanticism, so regional identities in architecture became more attractive. And in the late 19th century as high-style historicism exhausted itself, so regional identities in architecture and design became more evident, more elemental and more prophetic.

Scotland has imported many architectural styles and made them Scottish

St. Peter's Seminary at
Cardross by Gillespie,
Kidd and Coia (above),
St. Mungo's Museum of
Religious Art in Glasgow
by Ian Begg (right)

Nor is this creative resolution or fusion of the national and the international affected by some impersonal agency or 'force majeure'. There is plenty of evidence to show that such design has a deliberate, self-conscious, cultural intention. Mackintosh, for instance, referred approvingly to a specifically Scottish approach to architecture 'coming to life again' and calls for 'a code of symbols accompanied by traditions which explained them'. His aims were thoroughly explicit. Or Plecnik, ultimately committed to the creation of a valid Slovenian architecture between the Germanic and Italianate edges, was already writing in 1902 that 'Like a spider, I aim to attach a thread to tradition, and beginning with that, to weave my own web'.

There is nothing disreputable and certainly no creative dead-end in the 'conscious attempt to imbue architecture with a national characteristic'. To advocate otherwise would be to commend the imposition of a deracinated, First World, cultural imperialism. But neither is there any guarantee that this will lead to good architecture. Being at the edge makes the attempt to resolve the dialectic of time and place a particularly precarious path to follow. There are pitfalls to be avoided.

At one extreme, one might cite the later 20th century work of Gillespie, Kidd and Coia, of which perhaps St Peter's Seminary at Cardross might stand as an example. This is without question a 'building of distinction'; probably one of the most remarkable pieces of architecture built in Scotland in the 20th century. Tragically abandoned after less than a generation, its salvation is overdue. But this is an architecture obsessed with the international, wholly in thrall to 20th century developments in the history of art and architecture, to the extent that it seems without regard for indigenous tradition and climate. It is an architecture that denies the edge because it wants so much to be at the centre.

At the opposite extreme is much of Ian Begg's architecture as, for example, Glasgow's Museum of Religious Art. This too, in its way, is a 'building of distinction'. But it is an architecture obsessed with the national, wholly in thrall to the geography of art and architecture, to the extent that there appears to be nothing but a national tradition - and one unaffected, it seems, by two or three centuries of history. It is an architecture that wants to belong to the edge, denying the influences emanating from the centre.

If these are the pitfalls, what can be recommended? Responding to this appeal is itself a risky business, almost as precarious as actually resolving in design the conflicting claims of the national and the international. But for those designers or critics, who feel the cultural compulsion to respond to the imperative of identity, there is no escape from the obligation to declare the intent and run the risk of getting it wrong. Of those few - all too few - buildings that might be regarded

Church at Knockando in Moray by Law and Dunbar-Naismith (right), The Grianan Building, Dundee by Nicoll Russell (left), Benson & Forsyth's extension to the Museum of Scotland, Edinburgh (bottom),

as valid signs of the times and of the place, some are worthy of mentioning. Benson & Forsyth's extension to the Museum of Scotland in Edinburgh; Nicoll Russell's work at the Grianan Building, Dundee; and a Church at Knockando in Moray by Law and Dunbar-Naismith.

These examples may not necessarily be great pieces of architecture nor do they represent the only acceptable approach to the site. However, each is a 'building of distinction' and each is imbued in some way with a national or regional character. What makes them so may have something to do with materials and texture, but more importantly, results from the transformation of form. There is a kind of language of national form, not only distinct and recurring formal elements, but a syntax derived from such forms. Geometry, freed from its original materials and function, paradoxically still acts as a symbolic mediator of regional or national culture. It is this 'geographical geometry' that the design of these buildings employs.

Not everyone will be convinced by the view that 'to imbue architecture with a national characteristic' is wholly successful. There is, however, a certain danger about exemplars, for valid design needs to be thoroughly modern and of its time, whilst being part of a living tradition (of its place). What is wanted is an ambivalent architecture - or, rather, an ambi-valent architecture: one able to absorb these contending forces of time and place in the creation of new places in the 21st century.

References

Robertson & **Frampton:** 'Raising a Challenge', in Prospect , No. 54, Edinburgh, 1995, p. 9

Frampton Kenneth: Modern architecture and the critical present, Architectural Design, 1982

Inglis, J: 1868, quoted in Davie, G. E., op cit., p. 323

Mackintosh, C. R., 1891, quoted in Walker, F. A., 'Scottish Baronial Architecture' in

Robertson, P: (ed.), Charles Rennie Mackintosh, the Architectural Papers, Wendlebury Edinburgh, 1990, pp. 45-44

Masson, D: 1852 quoted in Davie, G. E.,. The Democratic Intellect, Edinburgh, 1982 (1961), p. 317

Pevsner, N: The Englishness of English Art, Harmondsworth, 1964 (1956), pp. 15-25 and passim

Plecnik, J: 1902, quoted in a review by Long, in Journal of the Society of Architectural Historians, Vol. 54, No. 1, Philadelphia, 1995, p. 99

Scott, P. H: In Bed with an Elephant, Saltire Pamphlets, New Series No. 7, Edinburgh, 1985

Smith, G: 1919, quoted in introduction by Buthlay, K., to MacDiarmid, H., A Drunk Man Looks at the Thistle, Edinburgh, 1987, p. 23

David Taylor
& Anthony Alexander

Understanding
Places

Peace and Winter Gardens,
Tyne Quayside & South Bank

Space, Place, Life is The Academy of Urbanism's motto. While space is objective and measurable, and life refers to the dynamic process of people in action, place is where the physical and the social combine. Places are formed by the physical stuff of brick and concrete on the one hand, and people's social needs and subjective experience on the other. In the previous volume of Learning from Place, Sarah Chaplin rationalised the study of place by defining place as process, place as experience and place as project. The process and experience represent the social function of a place such as a transport interchange, a market or a park. These functions and peoples' experience of them are clear indicators of quality. A good market or a good station produces a more positive experience than a bad one. The third aspect – place as project – refers to the way that places are created and managed.

The Academy's first selection for Great Places illustrated these themes in various ways. Brindleyplace in Birmingham was highly successful as a project that turned a derelict canalside district to a fully let, active, mixed-use business quarter within ten years. As a project, the developer, Argent, has taken responsibility for the ongoing management of the area. Borough Market in London has had a social function as a food market for hundreds of years. Originally, as a project, it served the purpose of paying for the cost of maintaining

Good places to spend time; The South Bank (top), outside the Winter Gardens (middle) and Newcastle Quayside (bottom)

Inside the Sage Gateshead (left) and a view from the Peace Gardens towards the Winter Gardens in Sheffield

London Bridge. Today, run by a charity, the place shifted its focus from a wholesaler to an upmarket 'gastro-centre' – place as experience – place as process. The third choice, St. Stephen's Green in Dublin, preserved its essential function as a relaxed, green lung at the heart of the city. As a project, the place has preserved its tranquillity despite the surrounding traffic.

To these three, the Academy now adds the Peace and Winter Gardens in Sheffield, the Newcastle-Gateshead Quayside and London's South Bank. Each of these places has been the result of major regeneration, demonstrating the urban renaissance of British cities in a post-industrial age. This essay attempts to show how the experience of these places today, the process that they serve and the projects that led to their creation illustrate ideas about how the nature of a place changes over time.

The character of each is influenced by the historical development of their parent cities. The experience of these places today is due to changes in the nature of the three cities over the last few decades and, more recently, the projects to change their development and management. The story of each city and their roles as part of the nation cannot be separated from the story of these specific places.

The fundamental nature of both London and New-castleGateshead is as the site of bridges over a river at a point near to the open sea. Both were subject to major development by the Romans some two thousand years ago. The City of London lies on the high ground of the north bank of the river, at the first point upstream where a bridge could be created. As such, the life of the city originated from the trading cluster developing around the intersection of road and river. For the Tyne too, the same dynamic applied, amplified by the Emperor Hadrian, with a vast wall stretching coast-to-coast like the Great Wall of China to create a transition point at which goods could be controlled and taxed.

Sheffield, by contrast, was a city built on a different relationship to water. The process that defined Sheffield was the natural hydro power pouring down from the Pennines that drove the mill wheels of early manufacturing. The geology of the region also yielded minerals, making Sheffield a centre for metalworking since the Middle Ages, and later the birthplace of steel. The city is right to pride itself on inventing a substance of such immense significance in the modern world.

All three cities were subject to intense development during the Industrial Revolution. Sheffield expanded tenfold during the 19th century. London and NewcastleGateshead became vast centres for commerce, manufacturing and shipbuilding. Each worked to amplify the strength of the other, extending the reach of the British Empire. The importance of their economic power meant each city was a major target during the Second World War. As such, their character in the latter part of the twentieth century was of inner city areas rebuilt with the post-war urbanism ideas of large-scale road infrastructure, high-rise housing and the separation of residential, employment and retail uses into dedicated zones.

Today, we celebrate each of these places as a great success precisely as a demonstration of the reversal from their state of decline in the latter half of the 20th century. As regeneration projects, London's South Bank, the NewcastleGateshead Quayside and Sheffield city centre, are all the result of change from industrial to post-industrial. The project to revitalise these three places has helped bolster civic pride and reverse the psychological feeling of a city in decline. The results allow these cities to be experienced in new ways in terms of both physical form, industrial heritage and cultural life.

Seeing these changes through has required the vision of local politicians, planners and partnership with private interests. Each has seen high levels of investment focused on improving the public realm through attractive design and the creation of new pedestrian routes. This focus on a high-quality walking and cycling experience marks a radical break from the post-war ideas of city engineers, planners and architects who, led by the likes of Abercrombie and Buchanan, put cars first and people second. The result of the car-based urbanism of the post-war period was higher mobility for traffic, until levels

expanded beyond even the capacity that had been planned for, and changes to the traditional movement routes of the cities produced a dysfunctional experience for those not in cars. Instead, removing the dominance of the motorcar returns the function of the city to the human, 'pedestrian' experience and clears the environment both of toxic particles and greenhouse gases. There is no doubt that a carbon-free city is the only meaningful vision for their future. And places for people are essential to ensure that the city invites economic and social activity rather than repelling it.

The masterplan for the Festival of Britain held in 1951 (facing page), the GLA building by Norman Foster (left) and the popular Jubilee Walkway created in 1977 (above)

The South Bank

The oldest of these places, London's South Bank, began with the post-war Festival of Britain in 1951, a showcase of a new society being built on the ruins of the old. Today, it is one of the most popular parts of London, and continues to evolve. The recent refurbishment of the public realm around the Royal Festival Hall has reinvigorated the South Bank. The former service areas behind the building are now also reborn as public spaces, and new pedestrian links back from the riverfront are now opening up parts of the London Borough of Southwark to growth as distinctive areas of the city. Fifteen million people pass along the South Bank every year, with arts, theatre and food providing destination points both on the riverside and immediately behind it.

The South Bank had always been industrial land. Wharves and warehouses were the economic powerhouses of the city and the function of the river was as an economic asset – a transit route. Abercrombie's plan for the post-war reconstruction of London noted that 73% of the riverside from Hammersmith to Wool-

wich was used by industry while only 12% was public open space. The plan noted, 'Some of the riverside properties are in a dilapidated condition owing to previous neglect and decay; others have been destroyed or damaged through enemy action; a number do not exploit the land occupied to anything approaching its maximum potentialities.' The proposal was to change these proportions such that public access to the river was increased by an additional 30%, wharves and warehouses reduced from 31% to 16%. Businesses and accommodation were slowly attracted in, aided in part by the Clean Air Act of 1956 that removed the acrid smoke that hung over London.

The Royal Festival Hall was the main 'legacy' structure from the Festival of Britain. The festival was largely accommodated in temporary structures, some on the long-barren Jubilee Gardens. Later, the National Theatre, National Film Theatre and Hayward Gallery followed, the former a deliberate attempt to create a public arts facility that broke with the past of West End showbiz theatre as

South Bank figure ground plan

THE SOUTH BANK

As I strolled down by South Bank way
One evening in July
My senses were bathed as the ambience caught
My mind, my ear, my eye;

The lights by the glowing River Thames
The skateboards' rattling dance,
The buildings waiting to tell me tales
Of promise and romance;

A stroll along the South Bank's buzz
By the laughter and night-lit faces
Reminds me of the power of stone and water
To combine in mystical places.

Shad Thames linking Tower Bridge to the Design Museum

much as its modern architecture broke with the traditional pillars and porticos of neo-classical London. The strategy that emerged for the South Bank was a precursor to the recent arts-led regeneration strategy for Gateshead.

Two clear lessons can be drawn from the South Bank, and its comparison with the similar riverside regeneration along the Tyne. Firstly, the South Bank shows the time it can take for a place to mature. It is large and links many distinct places yet it has taken half a century for Abercrombie's dream to be fully realised. To the east, destinations include the Design Museum, Tower Bridge and HMS Belfast; moving westwards, the more recent additions of the Tate Modern and Shakespeare's Globe, then the Oxo Tower and Gabriels Wharf. Finally, the heart of the South Bank lying around the Royal Festival Hall is revitalised by two new pedestrian bridges, and now includes, opposite the Houses of Parliament, the immensely popular London Eye, completed in 2000. Each of these places is linked into one whole only because of a long-term and loosely defined strategy.

In 1977, the Silver Jubilee Walkway was created to link various London attractions throughout the City and West End. It also included the route along the South Bank from Lambeth Bridge to Tower Bridge. People's natural desire to walk along the river brought the life that gave an economic rationale to produce further destinations along the length of the South Bank and improve the public realm along the route.

The second lesson is that, although specific physical interventions have created major destinations that pull people along the riverside path, the real joy of the South Bank is the emergence of unplanned activities along the way. The

The GLA Building looking towards Tower Bridge and two views of the Coin Street area developed by Coin Street Community Builders

route from the Eye to the Royal Festival Hall has become a promenade for street performers from living statues to acrobatic break-dancers. Fans of free-jumping have spontaneously gravitated to nearby areas and the Hayward's geometric under- croft is filled with life as an unintentional skateboard and BMX arena – functions wholly unanticipated by their architects.

The book market underneath Waterloo Bridge is a further example, benefiting from the protection the bridge provides from the rain, while other bridges provide acoustics that attract saxophone players and opera singers. These all point to the fact that architects and designers must expect the func- tion of a building or space to change, and that uses will appear that the designers are unable to imagine.

Below the civil engineering of the river-wall, at low tide a beach emerges below the South Bank that has hosted environmental campaigns on the plastic polluting our seas, sand sculptures and even late- night raves that go on until the river itself calls time. The South Bank is an endless demonstration of the emergence of creativity, not by design, but by spontaneous evolution.

Accommodating change is an essential attribute of our towns and cities that became lost in the Mod- ernists' belief in form following function. How would this make sense when function inevitably changes over time? Perhaps with hindsight this is too easy a point to make. In the wake of war, the reality of Britain's industrial demise had not yet sunk in. Now from the perspective of a post-industrial era, it is clear that adaptability is critical for buildings and the spaces between them. Change in the nature of place is inevitable and so the act of master-plan- ning, with strategic goals to be achieved over de- cades, must recognise the need to accommodate fuzziness whilst maintaining a clear goal.

Living sculptures and merry-go-rounds around the Millennium Wheel.

The Gateshead Millennium Bridge otherwise known as the 'Winking Eye Bridge' designed by Wilkinson Eyre

Newcastle Quayside

For NewcastleGateshead, a similar evolution of spontaneous place-making along the riverfront can be expected for the decades ahead. Like the Thames, the Tyne now hosts festivals and other temporary events that bring these places to life. The purpose of the river in both these cities is no longer as a route for trade and industry, but is a place for leisure and culture - for spectacles such as the Tall Ships Festival, or the Fish Festival (the Tyne is a salmon river), the annual Great North Run or even art installations such as Spencer Tunick's Naked City.

In both London and NewcastleGateshead, the interface between the two sides of the river, and a defining feature of the rebirth of these places, has been the footbridges constructed to mark the Millennium. Although a footbridge may appear a humble gesture, the new movement routes opened up have again shown that it is people that bring economic energy and life to a place. In both London and NewcastleGateshead these bridges create routes and

links to new cultural venues. Just as the cities as a whole have been shifting from an industrial economy to a knowledge economy, at the scale of individual buildings, flour mills and power stations are reborn as modern art galleries that bring the engines of the knowledge economy – people – into the cities. Both also show the pre-eminent importance of movement by people on foot.

The instantly iconic design of the Gateshead Millennium Bridge creates a visual harmony of curves complementing the steel lines of the Tyne's existing iconic bridges. The whole cityscape is reframed and the curvature of computer-aided design now complements the Victorian skyline. The aesthetic experience of this place is the perfect inspiration for future generations of engineers and architects.

History explains the present nature of the two cities. In 1854, a fire in Gateshead's warehouses storing coal and other chemicals caused a catastrophic

QUAYSIDE , NEWCASTLE

Pardon ? You what ? I can't hear you
For the music and the laughter
Loud lights on the water
And the Tyneside sons and daughters
Living for today and hoping for tomorrer
And if you want energy...
You can come here and borrer!

Say again ? Yes, a river runs through it
Like a River of Life if you'll let me have a cliché
Like a River of Words if you're feeling canny
Like a River of Laughter from each nook and cranny
Like the tide's in and you want to splash in it
And the night's an adventure and you want to begin it!

Pardon ? You what ? I can't hear you
For the sound of an enormous ringing Aye!
As life is embraced by the water's edge
And you feel the Quayside beginning to fly...

Newcastle Quayside figure ground plan

explosion that completely destroyed the medieval streets along both sides of the river. Newcastle rebuilt its side of the river, whereas Gateshead did not. This explains why in Newcastle there is a natural route down from its railway station on the ridge of the valley, past fine Victorian buildings to the quayside below. In Gateshead, the town centre lies some way to the south and the riverfront became cut off.

By the 1960s, the Tyne had become a vacant backwater. Both cities had effectively turned their backs on the river. The quayside went from being a centre to a periphery, and only with the recent regeneration has the Tyne become a centre again. The first plans to achieve this had been developed by Newcastle City Council in the early 1980s, but it was not until the creation of the Tyne and Wear Development Corporation in 1987 that an economic strategy began to be put in place. With powers of land assembly and planning, the development corporation prompted major quayside projects such as the four-star Copthorne Hotel and high-quality office and residential conversions in listed Victorian buildings.

The steep topography of the Tyne valley made master-planning complex and reinforcement of the river wall was a prerequisite for any significant development. Further refurbishments and new buildings followed, bringing a new flavour of economic activity to the quayside. Residential apartments and bars started to bring new life to the area and pull activity from the city centre above down to the riverside.

With Newcastle and Gateshead in separate political authorities, Gateshead long being part of the jurisdiction of the City of Durham to the south, different strategies took place on each bank. In Newcastle,

The steep-sided valley and its bridges make Newcastle Quayside one of the most dramatic urban environments in the UK

View through the 'Blinking Eye Bridge' to the Baltic Flour Mill, now the BALTIC Centre for Contemporary Arts

the economics-led strategy sought to refurbish the historic buildings and open new land for development. On the other hand, Gateshead's approach was based on responding to the evidence that the local population had the lowest levels of arts attendance in the UK. The arts-led strategy was started by commissioning Antony Gormley's Angel of the North, clearly visible by road and rail to the south of Gateshead. Two key venues followed: The Baltic – the only international art venue between London and Edinburgh – and the Sage Gateshead, a world-class concert venue. In tandem, the two cities have been frequently voted England's top city break destination. Tourism alone is now worth £800 million to the local economy. People can enjoy an evening out, view modern art and take in a concert, creating the cosmopolitan air that encourages creative people to stay and set up business.

But visitors to Newcastle are not yet led through coherent routes informed by a large-scale masterplan. People can naturally make their way down from the railway station to the riverside, along enigmatic stairways that seem hewn into the rock of the valley walls.

Across the river, with Gateshead city centre lost beyond 1960s dual carriageways, the Sage, Baltic and high-rise apartments of the Quayside stand alone with, as yet, nothing else around but car parking; the visitor is therefore pulled back over the river to Newcastle, across either of the bridges. As London's experience has shown, the creation of new attractors will pull people along the shoreline. Increased circulation of people around the valley floor will ultimately mean new development on both sides of the Tyne, and ultimately an enhanced relationship between the two cities.

Sheffield Peace and Winter Gardens

Sheffield is also a great engineering city but the change in its fortunes tells a different story from that of NewcastleGateshead. The biggest change to the city centre came from the movement patterns created by the car-based society emerging in the second half of the twentieth century. First, the central shopping area had become landlocked by the post-war ring road system, the outer ring of which became a hinterland of warehouses increasingly prone to abandonment in the 1980s. Secondly, the Meadowhall shopping mall, opened in 1990, undermined the role of the city centre as a retail space. Sheffield had to re-evaluate its essential purpose. Where the new mall would inevitably outperform the city centre in terms of retail, it would never provide the civic space, the town hall, library, gallery and museums that remained as testaments to the city's great past.

The Heart of the City project began in 1997 with the objective of refreshing the public spaces of the city centre. By 2000, this had expanded into a plan to create major new pedestrian routes. What has now been created in the city is an extremely high-quality pedestrian experience, connected by 'The Gold Route' that links the railway station at the valley floor to the city centre on the hillside above, via a series of new public spaces. From the new station forecourt, across traffic-calmed Arundel Gate, this route leads to the Millennium Galleries and the Winter Gardens' spectacular timber and steel glasshouse, through the re-vitalised Peace Gardens to Barker's Pool in front of the City Hall, now redesigned to better accommodate large public gatherings such as New Year's Eve celebrations.

The route was made possible by a number of interventions including the removal of the post-war extension to the Town Hall: a bland concrete oblong nicknamed 'the egg box' that blocked one side of the Peace Gardens. Along the length of the route, the road network needed substantial alteration, requiring not only the foresight and leadership of the politicians and planners responsible, but also the co-operation of a wide range of local landowners. Two 1960s high-rise blocks were demolished, the A61 downgraded and Howard Street pedestrianised.

As with the Thames and the Tyne, the public spaces created have become venues for temporary events ranging from formally managed spectacles, such as converting the Peace Gardens into a beach, to

The Winter Gardens (facing page) and a view from one of the new cafes towards the Peace Gardens in Sheffield

Peace and Winter Gardens figure ground plan

PEACE AND WINTER GARDENS, SHEFFIELD

Like those flowers that seem to shoot up overnight,
Reshaping the landscape, defining the view,
These gardens have grown and enfolded the light
In places that seem like they shout: We are new!

Let's not forget that this place could have rusted,
Could have laid down and died, turned to the wall
But instead a proud city's future's entrusted
To places that bustle from dawnbreak to nightfall;

And places like this are where cities take their time
And edge towards a working definition of sublime...

informal activities like local kung fu clubs training in the open air under the shade of trees. The benefits of the new movement routes and high quality public realm were extremely hard to quantify in advance. Yet justification was provided by the enthusiasm of the public consultation; 25,000 people offered their views, helping to create a sense of ownership in the regeneration process. The use of Pennine sandstone, stainless steel and water all anchor the streetscape design in the city's strong regional character and distinct industrial heritage.

A clear strategy for delivery and management ensured that each single project was seen as part of a greater whole. The active management of the spaces played a vital role, with the employment of street wardens, known as ambassadors, fundamental to

the success of the project, which is now inspiring similar schemes across the country. These public servants have a highly pro-active presence on the city streets, giving local residents, businesses and visitors someone to ask questions of, providing instant feedback to the authorities on maintenance issues and contributing to a sense of safety and security.

For Sheffield, the future challenge will be how the Heart of the City project will seem in 30 years time. How can it be ensured that the planning and investment made to create the specific interventions in the city survive into the long term? The value of large-scale investment will soon fade if there is a future failure of management or decision to cut back on operational expenditure.

As with London's South Bank, the central logic of the route (from the station to the centre) has been established, but the process of people moving along it and subsequent addition of further destinations on the route will emerge over many decades. The execution of Sheffield's regeneration through strategic planning, coherent design and ongoing management is exemplary. The city has successfully recaptured its role as a regional centre by creating an attractive public realm connecting a series of significant buildings. As an example of what urban regeneration can achieve and the elements required for such success, Sheffield provides a significant lesson for others.

The Gold Route in Sheffield runs from the station up Howard Street (middle bottom) through the Heart of the City redevelopment (middle above) and the Peace Gardens (right and left)

In all three places, the challenge is to keep the vision alive and ensure that the ups and downs of wider forces keep the options for change open rather than closed. The South Bank began with a vision in the 1940s that took until the 1970s to come together. Today, the situation is of ad hoc arrangements, fragmented ownership and no coherent control or management of the space. High quality materials used in the public realm have fallen into disrepair through lack of maintenance, which the management process enjoyed by Sheffield could have helped prevent. The nature of place, the confluence of objective space and subjective life, is always in a state of flux and change. The quality of a place begins with a smooth flow of people, attracted in because it serves a function, either for movement or as a destination, even if that function is just a pleasant or entertaining experience. Maintaining quality means ensuring that this flow is not blocked or cut-off and that the nature of the place is able to survive its changing context.

Simple lessons for achieving high quality places may be summarised as follows:

- Movement – Legible routes to destinations bring vibrancy, natural surveillance and economic vitality. Once established, routes can expand, opening up new quarters and future social and economic life.

- Investment – Invest in an ongoing management regime. Ongoing operational expenditure beyond short-term capital investment, such as with Sheffield's city ambassadors, is essential to maintain the physical quality of a place.

- Time – Places change over time. Changing demands, whether economic, demographic or the impact of global warming, all highlight the need to respond to an unknowable future, so adaptability is a critical design consideration.

- Spontaneity – Encourage and adapt to the spontaneous – The way in which spaces are used is the result of bottom-up spontaneous use by people, so masterplanning should seek to balance a formal, top-down vision with public consultation and an expectation of informal activity.

- Legibility – Visitors to a city rely on legible routes, either through how buildings are laid out or through signage and public maps. If existing routes are not well signposted they will only be used by people who already know where they are going.

- Accessibility – Whether through urban design that reflects the needs of wheelchair or pram users, the needs of the visually impaired or good routes for cyclists, high quality places should be accessible to all.

- Sense of place and civic pride – Geographical features such as a river, use of local materials and attention to industrial heritage or historic streetscape elements can all contribute to a high-quality place.

All three places are full of vitality: South Bank (above), Newcastle Quayside (left) and Sheffield (right)

Kevin Murray

Looking beyond the Object

In the years since its launch, The Academy of Urbanism has made continuous progress as a result of our core activity - presented in these pages - namely that of Learning from Place.

We have reviewed places where interesting things are happening, visited many locations of different scales to assess them for awards, and also looked in more depth at those places that have hosted our conferences and Annual Congress. So, in a relatively short time we have put the microscope over places as diverse as Belfast and Berlin, Ludlow and Liverpool, Malmö and Manchester, St. Andrews and St. Ives, as well as streets and neighbourhoods in London, Birmingham, Dublin, Edinburgh and Glasgow.

In the very early days, before the Academy really got going, there was some concern expressed by various parties about our potential role. What was to be our purpose? How would we be any different from CABE, the Urban Design Group, or the Urban Design Alliance? And how would we differentiate ourselves from the Academy of Sustainable Communities, newly launched by John Prescott? Surely we were just an arm of the RIBA, and therefore only really interested in urban design from an architect's perspective?

It is thanks to our diverse membership, as well as our sponsors and supporters, including many people from the places that we have visited, that we have grown into something completely distinctive. Something 'extra' - adding to the debate and thinking, the skills and techniques needed for good urbanism. We started out, for practical management purposes, aiming to have only one hundred invited Academicians, drawn from a diverse range of backgrounds. Importantly, although we had many architects, we also

Newcastle

interested developers, planners, landscape architects, academics and commentators. All were committed to a wider and deeper understanding of urbanism than was being achieved by current planning policy and site-by-site development. A government sponsored Urban Task Force was simply not enough; a deeper movement was necessary. To help achieve this, we wanted to stimulate a discourse about what worked and why, principally from places that positively sustain human life now – rather than starting from any single academic theory or professional liturgy, which we saw as potentially part of the problem of simplistic and failing urbanism.

Others saw different problems. Because some of our early award winners were drawn from places like Edinburgh and Ludlow, or Newcastle's historic Grainger Town, The Academy was perceived by some to be failing to meet early expectations and personal aspirations. This has provoked reflection. First – that we were not focusing enough on contemporary placemaking initiatives – particularly the work of leading design practitioners. The Academy's Awards, and therefore our culture and focus, was at risk of becoming too rooted in the historic, with older towns and neo-classical neighbourhoods seemingly favoured. This is simply not true – and many contemporary projects, such as Glasgow's 'New Gorbals', Exeter's Princesshay and even the 'new city' of Milton Keynes, have all been nominated in one category or another. They simply have not yet made it all the way through our voting and assessment processes. It is not the purpose of The Academy to support the avant garde design fraternity per se (others do that more than adequately); but neither is it our purpose to oppose change and modernity. We are more pragmatic than that. We support what works – and can work across generations. It would appear from the evidence of recent assessments that the places that work well combine modernity with historic elements – like Newcastle's Quayside or Sheffield's Peace Gardens. So there is no opposition to contemporary urbanism – but there needs to be clear evidence that it works successfully beyond the shock of the first season of fashionability.

Second – there has been a criticism from some of the more socially concerned commentators that we are 'rewarding nice places' that already have townscape assets, and probably wealth, prestige and community confidence to go with it. We are not validating the efforts of weaker places with greater challenges, but perhaps with important initiatives. There is no such bias. Who could claim that Brick Lane, one of our finalists, was elite or privileged? And the City of Glasgow – whose streets and neighbourhoods have featured – had one of the worst reputations as a city of social deprivation and post-industrial decay. No, it is what a location has done with its assets that matters – in making a more distinctive, convivial and sustainable settlement.

Third – there has been the related criticism that the awards process is merely 'a parlour game' – picking names of attractive places people can think of by 'buggins' turn'. This again is flawed, and indeed somewhat disrespectful to the nominators, the assessors, the voters and, most importantly, to those who live and work in these places and put in the time to explain their strategy, design and everyday management.

Any reading of the Learning from Place books should provide the clear evidence of a thoughtful and reflective examination of the lessons we have drawn from the nominees. These are lessons from which other neighbourhoods and places can learn and thereby help to enhance their own localities.

Evidence of success

What we have found we are learning from these reviews is layered and often complex, partly because our inquiry seeks to understand more than may be superficially evident. Undoubtedly there is the sheer physicality of place – and those of us from a spatial persuasion tend to pick up on these attributes immediately.

However, beyond the initial sensory appreciation of place, we can construct a deeper, more cognitive interpretation. We can investigate underlying templates of street structure and plot rhythm that enable and contain diverse activity over time. We appreciate the roles of individuals – whether developers, designers, politicians or planners – and how they may have influenced the creation of a place. We gain an insight into rules, bylaws, policies and codes as they have an impact on towns, areas and spaces – either in their initial establishment or subsequent renewal.

Crucially, we are learning that urbanism is not simply about design. Nor is it

Barcelona

even about urban design, for scalability of space is not the only issue for us to consider. The art and science of good placemaking is an informed and intelligent process, often including mistakes along the way. It can include fiscal mechanisms to secure community gains or ongoing management, or subtle subsidies that sustain diversity and affordability of space for a mix of activities, like artists or specialist shops and restaurants, as in Birmingham's Jewellery Quarter. The market is clearly important, but it is not necessarily 'king' in any red (or is that blue?) blooded sense. Creative interventions and public-private collaboration have been a key feature of most of the great places studied. An untrammelled development market – especially one exclusively devoted to immediate property sales – does not seem to deliver the long-term perspective and accumulation of value evident in successful places.

The endeavour, campaigning and constructive collaboration of key players – from whatever background – is another key ingredient emerging from those places that work. Networks of people who care, often very passionately, about their place is a most important learning point. When a generation of activists is lost, sometimes a place can go into a temporary decline that is difficult to rescue.

Our research clearly identifies that good design is very important – of buildings certainly, but also of the broader 'armature' of streets and spaces. From the metagrid of Barcelona to the new squares of Birmingham's Brindleyplace, the fusion of distinctive character with a sense of comfort and people-friendliness makes for longterm success. Set-piece civic landmarks and keynote buildings can play their part, but they may not save a place that lacks the wider humanistic assets.

The ability to adapt and evolve places over time is also an emerging learning point. That might tend to point us away from fixed architectural blueprints of megaschemes that cannot evolve beyond the first generation occupier. Yet that is what we seem still to produce. We have lost some of the adaptive skills of creative preservation and re-use, yet a proportion of conservation regularly features in those places whose urbanism is applauded, such as London's South Bank and St. Pancras Station.

... to the future ...

As some of these learning points emerge, the need for action becomes increasingly urgent. As we learn from conventions such as MIPIM at Cannes, the development sector at home and abroad is moving towards ever-grander schemes that 'commodify' chunks of our urban space as numbers on a balance sheet. Putting a signature architect's name on a planning application will not convert this into exemplary urbanism. The credit crunch may delay this inevitable wave, but the fact that much of the investment will come from overseas banks and sovereign funds begs the question as to whether they will be remotely interested in the actualities of space, place and life… so what is The Academy doing about spreading the important message?

In addition to continuing to assess and publish learning from our Awards locations, we are establishing a network of UniverCities – following a very successful Congress in Sheffield in May 2008. This is a network of places that combine academia, practitioners, the public sector and communities in learning about their own place in much greater depth over time – and disseminating that learning to a wider audience. Some of the research is generic, some targeted on themes – including coastal resorts, diversity and inclusion, new public spaces and branding and reimaging.

Developing 'knowyourplace', an interactive learning hub, alongside our own associated website will ensure learning gets out there to a wide variety of audiences. The intention is to grow this into a major open resource for academics, students and communities to get the key learning about effective urbanism mainstreamed within a much wider audience, breaking down professional and academic silos. Developing toolkits and techniques such as Urban X-Rays is a means to help groups explore, record and track their own places using comparable formats. This enables different layers and details of knowledge to be gathered, compared and analysed to help understand the processes and implications behind the more obvious facets of urbanism. And by holding events and conferences – both small scale learning events and larger symposia and debates, such as the Le Corbusier one at Liverpool in November 2008, alongside the RIBA Trust's exhibition of his work, our aim is to combine thoughtful contributions from across Britain and Ireland, as well as mainland Europe and beyond. We have already participated in successful conferences in Copenhagen, Dublin, London and Sheffield as well as study trips to Belfast, Edinburgh, Glasgow, Malmö and southern Italy. Lastly we are growing the membership of The Academy as more people become aware of its role, purpose and message. We have enlisted many friends and an increasingly diverse membership of those committed to quality urbanism - across a range of sectors and geographical areas. We see this growth continuing over the next few years.

Our activity task groups aim to focus our activity around specific goals, agreed inputs and outputs – to provide real material, findings, products and ideas, for a wider audience. This is set up within an overall business plan structure, which can seem a little corporate to the uninitiated, but is really a mechanism to ensure positive and purposeful participation from our growing membership and friends.

This is very much an ongoing and growing set of initiatives, and we appreciate the support of our members and sponsors. Much depends on the input, ideas and enthusiasm of these individuals. In addition, the learning also draws from the nature and calibre of the places and locations that are nominated and shortlisted for the Awards. This process is open to anyone – so please help by suggesting places in each category that you consider provide us with the opportunity for place-based learning. If there is one thing we have learned along the journey so far, it is that the making of successful, convivial places is too important to be left to designers and planners alone. This must not be a private play-pen for precious or precocious professionals. Success depends on the inclusion of informed and knowledgeable politicians, developers and investors, working with practitioners and the wider community. We hope this latest version of The Academy's Learning from Place will help meet some of the needs of all of these target audiences.

Old Compton Street, Soho, London

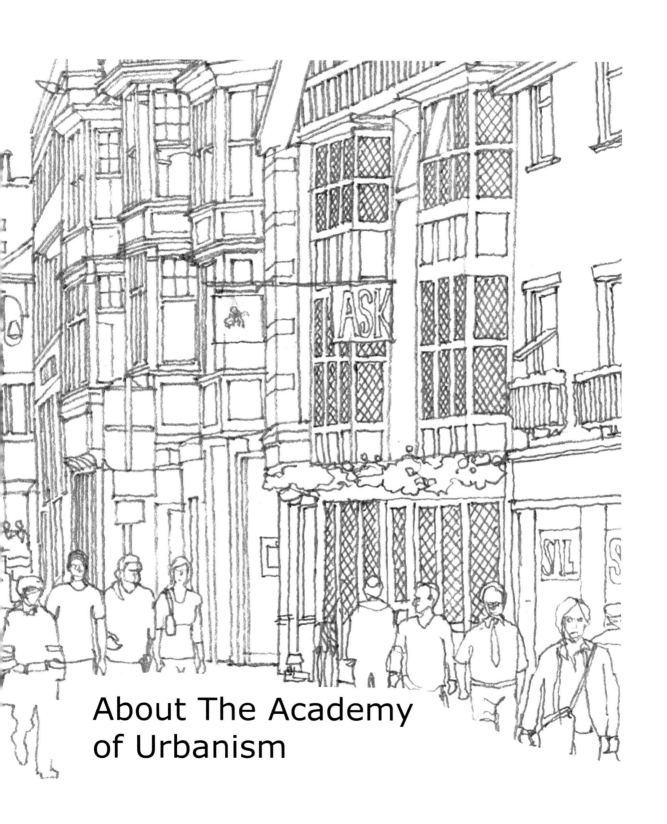

About The Academy
of Urbanism

Background

The Academy Manifesto

The Academy of Urbanism brings together a group of thinkers and practitioners involved in the social, cultural, economic, political and physical development of our villages, towns and cities, across Great Britain and Ireland. The Academy was formed to extend urban discourse beyond built environment professionals and to create an autonomous, politically independent and self-funded learned voice. We aim to advance the understanding and practice of urbanism by promoting a culture of scholarship through evidence-based inquiry, providing an inclusive forum for dialogue across all disciplines, sharing knowledge with the community and our peers and nurturing, recognising and rewarding excellence in achievement.

Principles

01 Successful urbanism is the result of a collective vision, realised through creative and enduring relationships between the community, government, developers and professionals involved in its design, delivery, governance and maintenance.

02 The culture, or cultures of the people and the ecology of the place must be expressed at a human scale and through both physical and social structures.

03 The identity, diversity and full potential of the community must be supported spiritually, physically and visually to sustain a sense of collective ownership, belonging and civic pride.

04 Vibrant streets and spaces, defined by their surrounding buildings and with their own distinct character, should form a coherent interconnected network of places that support social interaction and display a hierarchy of private, commercial and civil functions.

05 There must be a permeable street network with pedestrian priority that gives maximum freedom of movement and a good choice of means of transport.

06 Essential activities must be within walking distance and there should be a concentration of activity around meeting places.

07 Places must provide a diversity of functions, tenure, facilities and services; have a mix of building designs and types; and include a variety of appropriately scaled districts and neighbourhoods.

08 The social, cultural and economic needs of all inhabitants must be capable of being met without detriment to the quality of the lives of others.

09 Security should be achieved by organising the urban environment in ways that encourage people to act in a civil and responsible manner.

10 The pedestrian environment should be closely associated with active frontages at street level and there should be an appropriate intensity of use in all areas at all times.

11 The design of spaces and buildings should be influenced by their context and seek to enhance local character and heritage while simultaneously responding to current-day needs, changes in society and cultural diversity.

12 The public realm and civil institutions must be supported and protected by sound and inclusive processes that respond to the local community and changing economic and social conditions.

13 Decision-making for the ongoing development and management of the urban fabric must engage stakeholders and the local community through public participation and dissemination.

14 Diverse, accessible, affordable and active villages, towns and cities will encourage successful commercial activity, promote prosperity and support the well-being of their inhabitants.

15 New and existing places must respect, enhance and respond to their local topography, geology and climate and connect to the natural environment within and around them.

16 Urban parks and other landscaped areas should provide space for recreation, encourage biodiversity and help support a balanced environment.

17 New urban forms should be capable of adaptation over time to meet changing needs and to promote the continued use of existing resources, including the built environment.

18 The built environment must seek to minimise the use of carbon-based products, energy and non-renewable resources.

THE ACADEMY OF URBANISM

Where did it come from?

The Academy was launched in February 2006 and is a high-level, cross-sector group of individuals and organisations that champions, through discourse, research, education and awards, the cause of good-quality urbanism throughout Great Britain and Ireland.

The Academy seeks to promote and disseminate lessons about good urbanism and to work in partnership with other agencies and organisations that can assist in delivering best practice on the ground.

The concept grew from a core group of multi-disciplinary participants, brought together originally through the RIBA's Urbanism and Planning Group, with the intention of creating an Academy of one hundred people, to be renewed and updated over time.

What does it do?

Through its Academicians, the Academy promotes scholarship through evidence-based inquiry, fosters an inclusive environment for cross-disciplinary discourse, provides educational events focused on good urbanism, and validates good places and practice through The Urbanism Awards.

Who is involved?

The Academicians are drawn from a diverse range of professional, developer, academic and community backgrounds. Academicians are both enthusiasts and credible practitioners in their relevant fields, able to both help judge and disseminate lessons in good-quality urbanism. The culture of the organisation emanates from its Academicians, who are united in a committed obligation to share and disseminate their knowledge for the benefit of communities, villages, towns and cities.

How does it work?

Individuals become Academicians by invitation and pay an annual fee to belong to the Academy. In support of the Academy's Education Programme Academicians agree to initiate, or participate in, at least one 'badged' activity or event per year, promoting the practice and understanding of good urbanism. The Academy also publishes its own annual anthology, *Learning from Place*, drawing on its Awards programme as source material.

How does it fit with other bodies?

The Academy aims to fill a distinct role and not duplicate or contradict the primary roles of other bodies and organisations. It has links to other bodies, professions and the philosophical aspirations of others, and is supported by named representatives from a number of affiliated organisations. These currently include CABE, The Homes and Communities Agency, Architecture and Design Scotland, the Design Commission for Wales, RIBA, RIAI, South East England Development Agency (SEEDA), Yorkshire Forward, the Urban Design Group and the Urban Forum, Ireland.

The Academy is therefore not a completely stand-alone entity. It is a member-based network and is therefore different from the professions (RIBA, RIAI, RIAS, RTPI, RICS, etc.) who may share some of the same objectives, but who have a wider remit and are based upon technical entry levels and professional competencies.

The Academy is also different from CABE, as well as Architecture and Design Scotland and the Design Commission for Wales, in that it is not a government-created and funded body, but an independent network of key individuals and representatives.

Because of its cross-sectoral high-level voluntary network, the Academy is able to cut across professional and other boundaries, making connections between research, policy and the rhetorical aspects of advocacy and design, development, investment and implementation.

The Urbanism Awards

Through The Urbanism Awards, the Academy is creating a body of evidence-based research in Cities, Towns, Neighbourhoods, Streets and Places, that will be used, together with other exemplars, to further teaching, research and dissemination of best practice in urbanism.

Each year, the Academy shortlists three candidates in each category that are then visited, and studied thoroughly using the following criteria:

- Governance
- Local Character and Distinctiveness
- User Friendliness
- Commercial Success and Viability
- Environmental and Social Sustainability
- Functionality

Board and Academicians

Picture Credits

Cover Photo: Temple Bar crowds - **John Thompson**

All photographs except for those listed below taken by **John Thompson** during The Academy of Urbanism assessment visits.

All drawings created by **David (Harry) Harrison** and plans created by **Joe Wood**.

Page	Image	Credit
14	3 canals plan of Amsterdam	http://stock-images.antiqueprints.com
15	Cerdà's Plan of Barcelona	http://www.planum.net
15	Parc de Diagonal Mar	David Rudlin
16	Plan of Berlin	http://www.alt-berlin.info/
22	Barcelona Street	David Rudlin
28	Icaria Avenue in Barcelona	Charlie Baker
45	Ped Pocket drawing	Peter Calthorpe
49	Kilkenny festival	Kilkenny Borough Council
73	My Osaka maps	Courtesy John Worthington
76	Public Realm Plans	Steven Smith, formerly DEGW now Urban Narrative
101-7	Photos	David Rudlin
108	Wates Homes	Courtesy Wates Group Limited
120	Regent Street	Crown Estate
136	St. Peter's Seminary	Andy Haslam
136	St. Mungo's Museum	http://www.planetware.com/
138	Grianan Building	Nicoll Russell Studios
138	Knockando Church	LDN Architects
143	Festival of Britain Masterplan	http://sites.google.com/site/tombower sites/festival-of-britain-1951